INCREASING
YOUR PERSONAL CAPACITY

Pastors Eddie and Tammy Windsor

Champion Life Church
PO Box 1725
Rancho Mirage CA 92270

www.championlifechurch.com
info@championlifechurch.com

EDDIE WINDSOR

insight
PUBLISHING   GROUP
Tulsa, Oklahoma

INCREASING YOUR PERSONAL CAPACITY

Increasing Your Personal Capacity by Eddie Windsor
Published by Insight Publishing Group
8801 S. Yale, Suite 410
Tulsa, OK 74137
918-493-1718

Unless otherwise noted, Scripture quotations are from the New King James Version of the Bible. Copyright © 1979. 1980, 1982 by Thomas Nelson Inc., publishers. Used by permission. Scripture quotations marked TLB are taken from The Living Bible. Copyright © 1971 by Tyndale House Publishers, Inc. Used by permission. Scripture quotations marked NIV are taken from the New International Version, copyright © 1973, 1978, 1984 by International Bible Society. Passages marked KJV are from the King James Version. Scripture quotations marked NAS are from the New American Standard Bible. Copyright © 1960, 1962, 1963, 1968, 1971, 1972, 1973, 1975, 1977, 1995 by the Lockman Foundation. Used by permission. Scripture quotations marked TEV are taken from Today's English Version of the Bible. Copyright © 1966, 1971, 1976. Used by permission. Scripture quotations marked ISV are taken from the International Standard Version New Testament: Version 1.1.2000 (Print on Demand ed.) (2 Cor. 9:8-11). Yorba Linda, CA: The Learning Foundation.

Copyright © 2004 by Eddie Windsor
Second Printing 2004
Over 11,000 in print
All rights reserved.

ISBN: 1-930027-22-2

Library of Congress catalog card number: 2003105549

Printed in the United States of America

Here's What Christian Leaders Are Saying About *Increasing Your Personal Capacity* and Author, Eddie Windsor

Eddie Windsor's own life is an example of increasing one's Personal Capacity. Eddie is not only a great Christian, husband, father and friend, he's also a great life and ministry coach. I know this book will bless anyone who reads it.

Kevin Gerald
Senior Pastor, Champions Centre
Tacoma, WA

This book contains a powerful yet practical perspective on the potential and capacity of every human being. If you want more for your life, you'll be inspired and challenged by Eddie Windsor's fresh insights and biblical truths.

Brian Houston
Senior Pastor, Hillsong Church
Sydney, Australia

Eddie Windsor is uniquely gifted in helping both individuals and churches to enlarge their capacity. His mix of practical wisdom, theological soundness and contemporary wit make listening to his teaching and reading his writings a joy. If you want to take your life, family, business and ministry to the next level, then get your hands on *Increasing Your Personal Capacity* and devour every page.

Dr. Jim Reeve
Senior Pastor, Faith Community Church
West Covina, CA

I am excited about Eddie's new book entitled *Increasing Your Personal Capacity*. When he began to teach these principles in our church, it brought a fresh approach to personal growth. I love Eddie's commonsense approach to bringing forth these life-changing principles, and his track record proves an incredible wisdom in ministry. You won't ever look at your future the same way again once you have read this book.

Leon Fontaine
Senior Pastor, Springs Church
Winnipeg, MB CANADA

Eddie Windsor is on a mission to increase the Personal Capacity of everyone he comes in contact with. Finally he has brought his insights together in this fantastic book. Eddie's wisdom and down-to-earth leadership style is effectively helping leaders in every walk of life reach their full potential. I know you will enjoy this book! Better yet, apply what Eddie teaches and you will discover your dreams are only the "Next Level" away!

Rob J. Koke
Senior Pastor, Shoreline Christian Center
Austin, Texas

The stories and lessons in this book are simple and yet profound. You will be motivated to expand your capacity and experience fresh increase.

Bob Harrison
President
Christian Business Leaders International

DEDICATION

To Tammy, my best friend and the love of my life. Tammy, you are a wonderful wife and mother. I realize more every day that you have lifted my life. You bring out the best in me.

To my son Daniel, I want you to know I appreciate the sacrifices you have made and the countless hours on the road traveling with me from country to country. I will never forget our ministry trip to the Philippines, a real father and son adventure! I am proud of you son.

To my daughter Bethany, the joy of my life has been watching you grow into a beautiful young woman of God. You are God's amazing miracle, gift and joy of my life. You will always be beautiful in my eyes. No matter how old you are and even after you marry, you'll always be daddy's princess!

To my Mom & Dad, you have been the best parents a son could ever ask for. You have always believed in me and your constant encouragement to follow God's plan for my life has made me what I am today. You've helped me understand how I fit and how I could take my place in the plan of God. The most important thing you did for me was to show me how to fit in my local church and relate to my pastor.

To Mark & Linda Carpenter, you truly are lifelong friends and more like a brother to me. At times there were challenges in my ministry journey I didn't think I was going to be able to make it through, but I did because of your insight and encouragement. You lifted me so I could make it to the next level.

To Allen & Sharon Yadon, thank you for believing in me and embracing and loving our family the way you do. It is an honor to serve in the kingdom hand in hand with you. You are true friends!

Contents

PERSONAL CAPACITY

One evening, I was ministering in a church in Europe. At the end of the service, several people came up to the front of the church and asked me to pray with them about needs in their lives. I will never forget one particular man who asked me to pray with him about a job he had been believing God for. I asked the man what kind of job he desired. He said, "I want to have a top CEO management position that pays over two hundred thousand dollars per year plus perks." The man proceeded to tell me that he was faithful to his local church. He continued by saying, "I'm a tither, and I give regular financial offerings to my church." He surprised me when he quoted Proverbs 13:21, "The blessings of the Lord chase the righteous!" He said, "I have done all that I know to do, but I still have no answer to my prayer."

My initial thought was "This prayer is going to be easy!" But then I had the thought, "Ask the man what his management skills are." It seemed like a harmless thought. So I asked him, "Sir, what is your current level of management skills?"

He looked right at me and said, "I don't have any management skills."

At that moment, I thought I must have misunderstood him. So I decided to ask the question again in a little different way. "Sir, you are believing for an executive position requiring a high level of management skills. You will have many employees under your leadership. What is your current level of management skills?"

He looked right into my eyes and said, "I'm a tither, I'm a giver, I just need you to pray for me!"

I said to him, "Do you have any management skills?" He said no. I asked him where he was working now and what was his current pay. He said he worked in a local store as a sales checker and he made just over eight dollars per hour.

The dream you have in your heart for your marriage, your family, your employment, your church, and your life is being affected by your Personal Capacity.

It is hard to explain how I felt at that moment. I just stared into his eyes for what seemed like eternity. The truth is, I love what I do in the Kingdom of God! I believe in the power of prayer. I have seen over and over again God answer the prayers of His people. But to be perfectly honest, at that moment I wanted to quit. I tried to stay in faith, but when a man is standing before me, asking me to pray that he gets a job that I know he cannot handle, my faith just disappeared. Now is there anything wrong with working as a checker in a local store? No! That is a good job that would meet a person's needs. But can you see that the level of this man's current personal ability did not match the level of the resources he was asking of God?

Let's say a small glass of water represented this man's ability and a very large bucket of water represented the CEO management job. Do you know what would have happened if God had answered this man's prayer without considering his Personal Capacity? It would be like pouring the very large bucket of water into the small glass. Water would run out all over the floor and be wasted. Do you understand that the prayer this man was praying was being affected by his Personal Capacity?

I tried to encourage the man to follow his dream, but he would first need to become trained as a manager at his local store. That would seem to me to be the most logical place to start. But it was clear he was not interested in my thoughts. He just wanted God to do all the work, and he simply wanted to receive the benefits of the blessing.

Many of the answers to the prayers you are praying, right now at this time in your life, are being directly affected by the Law Of Capacity.

The experience I had that night talking to that man, sent me on a journey. I began to seek God for answers. Many of the concepts I will share with you about Personal Capacity came from that journey.

Several months later, I was reading a magazine article about people who had won millions by playing the lottery. They were horrible stories. The largest percentage of these people had not only lost all the lottery money, but in most cases, they were in a worse financial condition within a few short years. My initial thought was, "How is it possible to give someone millions of dollars, and it ruins their life?" Looking at it from my new capacity thinking, I realized how it could happen.

Most people who play and win the lottery have average-paying jobs, but when they win the lottery they are given millions of dollars; millions they do not have the capacity to manage properly. The money runs through their hands like water because they did not grow in character and ability to retain what they won. They simply were given all this money without going through the learning process on handling and valuing it.

Now let's look at the same scenario, but let's say Bill Gates won three hundred million dollars in the lottery. Now, according to our statistics, he would lose all the money in the next few years. However, I think most of us would agree that Bill has proven he would not lose the money. In fact, he would most likely double or triple the money he won. So what makes Bill different from the average person that wins the lottery? Capacity! It has been my observation that most people buying lottery tickets would not have the management skills to handle hundreds of millions of dollars, but the people that would have the capacity and skills would not consider wasting their money on lottery tickets.

Let's say we used a small cup to represent the size of a person's yearly income. It's easy to see that most of the water would be wasted on the floor if a person's cup size was fifty-five thousand dollars per year, but you tried to pour three hundred million dollars into their small cup.

As you read through the pages in this book, my prayer is that you would begin to understand that the dream you have in your heart for your marriage, your family, your job, your church, even your life, is being affected by your Personal Capacity.

CHAPTER 2

LAW OF CAPACITY

A few days ago, my wife, Tammy, and I got on an airplane and flew from London, England, to Vancouver, B.C. During that journey, a very important law was in effect the entire flight. It is called the Law of Lift and Thrust. The Law of Lift and Thrust enabled our airplane to lift off the runway—it carried us over the North Pole and brought us safely to our destination.

As Tammy and I sat on that airplane, we never thought once about the Law of Lift and Thrust, even though we were being affected by it the entire flight. It didn't matter if we understood this law. It didn't even matter if we believed in this law because it still affected our lives. In this chapter, we will talk about a law that most of us have been unaware of, but this law has affected each and every one of us every day of our lives! It is called the Law of Capacity.

Most people do not understand that the Law of Capacity is directly affecting their personal effectiveness.

In the book of Matthew, we gain valuable insight to identifying our present capacity and a pattern for increasing our Personal Capacity.

Matthew 25:14-29

For the kingdom of heaven is like a man traveling to a far country, who called his own servants and delivered his goods to them.

And to one he gave five talents, to another two, and to another one, to each according to his own ability; and immediately he went on a journey.

Then he who had received the five talents went and traded with them, and made another five talents.

And likewise he who had received two gained two more also.

But he who had received one went and dug in the ground, and hid his lord's money.

After a long time the lord of those servants came and settled accounts with them.

So he who had received five talents came and brought five other talents, saying, 'Lord, you delivered to me five talents; look, I have gained five more talents besides them.'

His lord said to him, 'Well done, good and faithful servant; you were faithful over a few things, I will make you ruler over many things. Enter into the joy of your lord.'

He also who had received two talents came and said, 'Lord, you delivered to me two talents; look, I have gained two more talents besides them.'

His lord said to him, 'Well done, good and faithful servant; you have been faithful over a few things, I will make you ruler over many things. Enter into the joy of your lord.'

Then he who had received the one talent came and said, 'Lord, I knew you to be a hard man, reaping where you have not sown, and gathering where you have not scattered seed.

And I was afraid, and went and hid your talent in the ground. Look, there you have what is yours.'

But his lord answered and said to him, 'You wicked and lazy servant, you knew that I reap where I have not sown, and gather where I have not scattered seed.

So you ought to have deposited my money with the bankers, and at my coming I would have received back my own with interest.

So take the talent from him, and give it to him who has ten talents.

For to everyone who has, more will be given, and he will have abundance; but from him who does not have, even what he has will be taken away.'

Have you ever wondered why the Lord gave different amounts of talents to each servant? At first glance, it looks as if there was some kind of discrimination or favoritism. But if we look at verse 15, we will find our answer.

Matthew 25:15

"And to one he gave five talents, to another two, and to another one, to each according to his own ability;"

So there was no discrimination that day. There was no favoritism that day. The Lord simply identified the preexisting abilities in each servant and matched the resource to his or her ability.

Servant number one had an ability of five, so the Lord matched his ability of five with a resource of five.

Servant number two had an ability of two, so the Lord matched his ability of two with a resource of two.

Servant number three had an ability of one, so the Lord matched his ability of one with a resource of one.

I remember the day I became aware of the Law of Capacity. It was then that I began to realize that God was not defining the size of my ministry. My ministry was being defined by my Personal Capacity. In 1997, when Tammy and I moved to the United Kingdom, God never gave us any indication what the size of our ministry would be. He gave us direction and a promise but no indication of the size. I believe the size of our ministry will be determined by our Personal Capacities.

The truth is that your employer does not define the success you have in the workplace. Ultimately, your success is defined by your Personal Capacity. Your spouse does not determine the quality of your marriage. Ultimately, it will be determined by your Personal Capacity.

The quality of your life is not determined by your sex, your gender, your skin color, your ethnic origin, your financial status, or even your geographic location.

Do you realize that your Personal Capacity is determining the quality of your life! There are two things you must understand about a Personal Capacity. First, every person on this planet has a Personal Capacity. And second, everything God gives you in this life has the ability for increase.

Have you ever heard it said, "The word of God is safe to build your life upon?" It's true! The Bible gives us patterns for living a full and successful life. There is an important pattern found in the Bible that gives us insights as to how to increase our Personal Capacity.

Let me give you the formula found in the book of Matthew for identifying one's Personal Capacity.

CAPACITY FORMULA:

MY ABILITY + MY RESOURCE + MY STEWARDSHIP = MY PERSONAL CAPACITY

Matthew 25:15a

"Gives us the resource"

"And to one he gave five talents, to another two, and to another one, to each according to his own ability"

Their resources came in the form of talents distributed by the Lord to match their personal ability.

Matthew 25:15b

"Gives us the ability"

"To each according to his own ability"

The abilities were preexisting in each servant that day. No ability was given out that day. Only the resources were given to match the preexisting abilities.

Matthew 25:16-18

"Gives us the stewardship"

> *Then he who had received the five talents went and traded with them, and made another five talents.*
> *And likewise he who had received two gained two more also.*
> *But he who had received one went and dug in the ground, and hid his lord's money.*

Stewardship is simply, what will you do with the resource God has given you?

Your Personal Capacity is determining the quality of your life!

I believe a person's resources in life are a reflection of their personal ability! Using a glass of water as an illustration, it's easy to see that the glass and the water are not the same thing. The glass represents "ability" and the water represents "resource." The glass gives me the ability to hold and use the resource. The same is true in your life. Your life becomes a container to receive and hold the resources of heaven. According to these Scriptures, the resources were given to match each servant's abilities, but stewardship was the deciding factor if there would be an increase or decrease in their Personal Capacity!

Most of God's people are praying for increased resources, but I believe we should be praying for an increased capacity!

The prayer of most believers today is, "Give me, give me, give me, my name is Jimmy!" They treat God as if he is a butler. They ring the bell and expect Him to come running to meet their every need. I believe we should pray less about money and do more praying for an increased ability. I love the prayer of Jabez for that very reason.

1 Chronicles 4:10

And Jabez called on the God of Israel saying, 'Oh, that You would bless me indeed, and enlarge my territory, that Your hand would be with me, and that You would keep me from evil, that I may not cause pain!' So God granted him what he requested.

Notice that Jabez is not asking God for more money. He is asking God for His blessing so that he could enlarge his territory or capacity. There are so many people praying the prayer of Jabez today! But they are praying half the prayer and getting half the results. Jabez prayed for God to bless him, but he also prayed for an increased territory or capacity.

> **When your abilities and your resources are given proper stewardship, an increased capacity will naturally follow.**

In Matthew 25, we find that ability came first, and the resources followed. But most people get the cart before the horse. They want God to provide the resource, then they will really be able to do something significant with their life. But that is backwards! We are making this thing way too hard. When your abilities and your resources are given proper stewardship, an increased capacity will naturally follow.

Every area of a person's life is affected by their Personal Capacity, even the prayers they are praying! The truth is that many of the answers to the prayers you are praying right now, at this time in your life, are being directly affected by your Personal Capacity!

CHAPTER

3

THE LAW OF CAPACITY AND PERSONAL PROPHECY

I believe every area of a person's life is attached to the Law of Capacity. An example of this would be Personal Prophecy. Let's look at an example from the life of David. One day, the prophet is instructed by God to go to the house of Jesse to declare whom He had picked to be the next King of the Nation. This is how Personal Prophecy works. God speaks to one of His ministers, instructing them to declare to someone what His desire is for their future.

2 Peter 1: 20-21(NASV)

But know this first of all, that no prophecy of Scripture is a matter of one's own interpretation, for no prophecy was ever made by an act of human will, but men moved by the Holy Spirit spoke from God.

So let's look at how Personal Prophecy affected the life of a young shepherd boy named David.

1 Samuel 16:8-13

So Jesse called Abinadab, and made him pass before Samuel. And he said, "Neither has the Lord chosen this one."

Then Jesse made Shammah pass by. And he said, "Neither has the Lord chosen this one."

Thus Jesse made seven of his sons pass before Samuel. And Samuel said to Jesse, "The Lord has not chosen these."

And Samuel said to Jesse, "Are all the young men here?" Then he said, "There remains yet the youngest, and there he is, keeping the sheep." And Samuel said to Jesse, "Send and bring him. For we will not sit down till he comes here."

So he sent and brought him in. Now he was ruddy, with bright eyes, and good-looking. And the Lord said, "Arise, anoint him; for this is the one!"

Then Samuel took the horn of oil and anointed him in the midst of his brothers; and the Spirit of the Lord came upon David from that day forward. So Samuel arose and went to Ramah.

What an awesome day that must have been for young David. He was chosen by God to be a King to lead His people. Now let's speculate for a moment what David's future might look like. Will they take him off to the palace? Will they begin to train him for his role as the future king? Will they replace his shepherd's clothes with a fine linen robe? Now, I cannot tell you exactly how much time will pass, but we do know that God's promise is out in David's future. And it seems that David is not getting any closer to the palace. Let's go forward in time to see what David's future is looking like.

1 Samuel 17:20

So David rose early in the morning, left the sheep with a keeper, and took the things (supplies) and went as Jesse had commanded him. And he came to the camp as the army was going out to the fight and shouting for the battle.

When a word comes to you in the form of a Personal Prophecy, it is speaking to your future Potential Capacity.

How is it possible for David to be given a personal word of prophecy by the leading prophet of his day that he would be the next King of the nation, but still be out watching sheep? Did the prophet miss it? Did David miss it? Or is there an explanation right before our eyes? At this point in David's life, he has the Potential Capacity to become a King. But he has the current ability to watch his father's sheep. The prophet spoke to his Potential Capacity and then sent him back to watch the sheep based on his current ability! Can I tell you the truth today? This is how prophecy can mess up good people. When a word comes to you in the form of a Personal Prophecy, it is speaking to your Potential Capacity! So David now had to go back, watch the sheep, and increase his current ability! Return to your regular duties in life with an understanding that it's time to increase your capacity. When the Word of the Lord comes to you in the form of a Personal Prophecy, it is speaking to your Potential Capacity.

It has been over twenty-two years since I started my ministry journey. I have watched this happen over and over again when a person receives a personal word of prophecy. So many people hear what their Potential Capacity is in the form of a Personal Prophecy, and they run off to ruin their lives.

Most people think the lion and the bear were trying to stop David from fulfilling his destiny, when the lion and the bear were his destiny!

Let's look again at the sequence of events in the life of young David. After receiving the word of prophecy did he go straight to the palace? No, he returned to his regular job watching sheep, which was his place of training. God had David on an important training program. A training program that would increase his capacity to the size of a King! His training started with doing simple tasks and chores for his father, Jesse. Believe me, doing chores at home was never fun or exciting for anyone! But finally David graduated to watching over the family flocks. Hardly a promotion these days! God had His way of stretching young David. First, David had to slay a lion. Then, he had to slay a bear. Finally, he slew a giant. David continually increased in his personal ability with each challenge he faced.

David continually applied stewardship to everything entrusted to his care. Through approximately a seventeen-year span of time, David finally became a King and the Prophecy was fulfilled. Most people think the lion and the bear were trying to stop David from fulfilling his destiny when the lion and the bear were his destiny!

If you receive a word of prophecy, then go back to work or your place of serving and apply stewardship.

This is the place where God will stretch you. He will grow you and will help you increase your capacity through the challenges of life and ministry. And if you do not run out on God's process or give up and quit, you too can have fulfilled prophecy in your life! A person must understand that personal words of prophecy are tied to their Personal Capacity.

CHAPTER
4

THE LAW OF CAPACITY AND THE GIVING OF TITHES AND OFFERINGS

Malachi 3:10

'Bring all the tithes into the storehouse, That there may be food (provision) in My house, And try Me now in this,' Says the Lord of hosts, 'If I will not open for you the windows of heaven And pour out for you such blessing That there will not be room enough to receive it.'

L et's break this verse down and look at it from the viewpoint of capacity. Every time you tithe, the windows of heaven are opened. It is important to understand that tithing is not like playing the lottery. Tithing is not about luck; it is not about playing the odds. Tithing is based on equality; it works the same for every person, every time. Most people do not understand that every time they give their tithe, the windows of heaven are opened.

First we need to establish something—is the Bible true? Yes, of course it is! Then how is it possible that every time I tithe, the windows of heaven open, and my

> **Every time a person gives their tithe, the windows of heaven are opened.**

checkbook still looks like it does? The bank has not called me lately, telling me, "Mr. Windsor, you have too much money in our bank, so could you stop depositing your money here!" So why does the Bible say that if we tithe, God will pour out such a blessing that we will not have room enough to contain it all?

I know thousands of people who tithe, and I don't know one person who does not continue to believe God for more increase. You have to admit something is not adding up here. But have we missed an important piece of the tithing principle? Remember what we just read in Malachi that you will not have room enough to receive it!

You will never have the capacity to retain all your tithing can produce!

The Bible clearly declares that when a person gives their tithes, the windows of heaven are opened and they cannot contain it all. If the Bible is true, and it is, then there is no way you can contain all that your tithing can produce.

Let me illustrate it like this. Let's use an eight-ounce cup to represent your current capacity. Sunday morning comes around, and you place your tithes in the offering plate. The windows of heaven open, and the blessing of God comes out. The blessing pours into your eight-ounce capacity until it overflows onto the floor, leaving you with eight ounces of resources and the extra water goes on the floor.

Let's say, over time, you increase your capacity to twelve ounces. The next Sunday morning comes around, and you place your tithes in the offering plate. The windows of heaven open and the blessing of God comes out. The blessing pours into your twelve-ounce capacity until it overflows onto the floor, leaving you with twelve ounces of resources and the extra water goes on the floor.

We will say you increase your capacity again to twenty ounces. The next Sunday morning comes around, and you place your tithes in the offering plate. The windows of heaven open and the blessing of God comes out. The blessing pours into your twenty-ounce capacity until it overflows onto the floor, leaving you with twenty ounces of resources and the extra water goes on the floor.

**You can never outgrow God's ability
to bring increase into your life!**

Can I tell you what I love about Malachi 3:10? That no matter how much a person is able to increase their Personal Capacity, God will always pour more into their life than they are able to contain. That is a good thing. I hope that you understand that you can never outgrow God's ability to bring increase into your life!

2 Peter 1:20 (NASV)

"But know this first of all, that no Scripture is a matter of one's own interpretation,"

All my life, I heard Malachi 3:10 taught like this: when you tithe, the windows of heaven are opened. Then your life is filled with so many resources that it begins to overflow onto everyone around you. This creates a blessing not only for you, but also for others around you. I know that is one way to interpret this Scripture, but I believe there is more to it.

Let's go back to our illustration. If your Personal Capacity is a twenty-ounce cup and you tithe, the windows of heaven open, filling your cup, and continuing to overflow onto the floor. Let me ask you a question. Is the water in your cup or the water on the floor a blessing to those around you? Can you imagine a person coming to you in their time of need and you saying, "God has truly blessed me, and you can have as much blessing off the floor as you want." What will truly bless the people around you? The resource held within your Personal Capacity, not the water that has spilled over onto the floor!

Tithing is your guarantee that you will always have provision in your life. How much provision you retain will be determined by your Personal Capacity.

Luke 6:38

"Give, and it will be given to you: good measure, pressed down, shaken together, and running over will be put into your bosom."

One more time, we see God's desire to pour blessing into our lives. We serve a big God. We serve a God who has more than enough resources to bless His people. He doesn't give us just a little blessing here and there, but a good measure, pressed down, and running over measure of resource.

2 Corinthians 9:8-11(ISV)

God is able to make every blessing of yours overflow for you, so that in every situation you will always have all you need for any good work.

As it is written, "He scatters everywhere and gives to the poor; his righteousness lasts forever."

Now he who supplies seed to the sower and bread to eat will also supply you with seed and multiply it and enlarge the harvest of your righteousness.

In every way you will grow richer and become even more generous,

Philippians 1:9 (NLT)

"I pray that your love for each other will overflow more and more, and that you will keep on growing in your knowledge and understanding."

Genesis 41:47 (NLT)

"After seven years, the granaries were filled to overflowing. There was so much grain, like sand on the seashore, that the people could not keep track of the amount."

Deuteronomy 28:5-6 (NLT)

You will be blessed with baskets overflowing with fruit, and with kneading bowls filled with bread.

You will be blessed wherever you go, both in coming and in going.

Psalm 23:5 (NLT)

"You welcome me as a guest, anointing my head with oil. My cup overflows with blessings."

Proverbs 3:10 (NLT)

"Then he will fill your barns with grain, and your vats will overflow with the finest wine."

Joel 2:24 (NLT)

"The threshing floors will again be piled high with grain, and the presses will overflow with wine and olive oil."

The dream you have in your heart for your family, your job, your church, and for your life is attached to your Personal Capacity!

CHAPTER 5

THE LAW OF CAPACITY AND MIRACLES

Often I minister in as many as three to five churches in a week. In many of those meetings, I pray for the needs of people, and I could tell you stories all day and night like the story I'm about to tell you. A man came up to the front to ask for prayer for a new job. He said that God had told him that he would know what job he was to accept when he talked to the right company on the phone. He said, "I have been waiting and waiting for that call, but it hasn't come yet. I know, that I know, that I know, I heard God tell me that the phone would ring!"

I don't know why I do things like this, but I thought I would ask him a question before I prayed for him. I asked him how many job resumes and/or job interviews he had made to get an idea of how many calls he would be expecting.

He said, "What do you mean?"

It did not sound like wisdom to me to sit by the phone and do nothing. I told him God would not do for you what you can do for yourself. I suggested to him to get out there and look for a job. It was apparent to me that he did not like what I had to say.

Several months later, I was back at that church for a second set of meetings. After one of the services, the man walked up to the front to tell me his story. He said, "You will never guess what happened after you prayed with me last time you were here. I left the meeting very angry with you, but after a few days of no calls for me to go to work anywhere, I decided to write some resumes and go to a couple job interviews. A few days later, several of the companies called, offering me work. And I knew exactly what offer to accept when they called me." Then the man said, "I wonder how long I would have sat by the phone if you had not made me mad."

Ephesians 6:13-14

Therefore take up the whole armor of God, that you may be able to withstand in the evil day, and having done all, to stand.
Stand therefore,

Notice it says, "Having done all." Most people do little, if anything, to stand. The mentality of far too many people today is whatever will be, will be. But God's Word shows us that we have a part to play. God will not do your job, and you cannot do His job. God will only do for you what you cannot do for yourself.

I call it the Natural Super-Natural Natural formula. The story of Elisha and the widow starts with a natural need. She has debts she cannot pay, so she goes to the man of God for help. Notice the man of God does not just pray that God would supernaturally answer the widow's needs. He gives her something to do in the natural to meet her need. Elisha told her to go borrow vessels and pour her resource of oil she had into the vessels.

The widow borrowed vessels as a way to increase her capacity to hold more resources.

As soon as she moved forward in the natural, the supernatural took over and filled every vessel. The borrowing of vessels was an act of increasing her capacity to hold more resources. Notice that when the vessels were full and there was no more room to contain more resources, the supernatural miracle ceased. I want you to notice something—when the supernatural was over, the widow now had a lot more oil, but she still had no money to pay her debts. God did not pay her bills for her. Once the supernatural was over, it was back to the natural. She had to go sell the oil in the market place to pay her own debts. God only did for the widow what she could not do for herself, but He still required her to do the things that she could do for herself.

Natural Super-Natural Natural

2 Kings 4:1-7

A certain woman of the wives of the sons of the prophets cried out to Elisha, saying, 'Your servant my husband is dead, and you know that your servant feared the Lord. And the creditor is coming to take my two sons to be his slaves.'

So Elisha said to her, 'What shall I do for you? Tell me, what do you have in the house?' And she said, 'Your maidservant has nothing in the house but a jar of oil.'

Then he said, 'Go, borrow vessels from everywhere, from all your neighbors—empty vessels; do not gather just a few.

And when you have come in, you shall shut the door behind you and your sons; then pour it into all those vessels, and set aside the full ones.'

So she went from him and shut the door behind her and her sons, who brought the vessels to her; and she poured it out.

Now it came to pass, when the vessels were full, that she said to her son, 'Bring me another vessel.' And he said to her, 'There is not another vessel.' So the oil ceased.

Then she came and told the man of God. And he said, 'Go, sell the oil and pay your debt; and you and your sons live on the rest.'

Many people are sitting around waiting for God to bail them out of debt with a supernatural miracle. Once this widow increased her capacity, God filled that new capacity with matching resources. I believe we must first move forward in the natural, increasing our Personal Capacity before God will move in the supernatural, increasing our resources to meet the needs we have in our life.

CHAPTER

6

THE LAW OF HARD

I don't know about you, but sometimes it seems like life gets a little hard. I have faced circumstances in life, ministry, and business that I thought I would never be able to overcome. At times, I have felt so much mental pressure I could actually feel my knees starting to buckle. Life has a way of becoming hard at times. But I have found a way to help myself through those hard places. I call it the Jethro Formula. The Jethro Formula simply helps me organize my thoughts so I can walk out from under the pressure.

The Jethro Formula

Exodus 18:13-18 (NLT)

The next day, Moses sat as usual to hear the people's complaints against each other. They were lined up in front of him from morning till evening.
When Moses' father-in-law saw all that Moses was doing for the people, he said, 'Why are you trying to do

*all this alone? The people have been standing here all
day to get your help.'*

*Moses replied, 'Well, the people come to me to seek
God's guidance.*

*When an argument arises, I am the one who settles
the case. I inform the people of God's decisions and teach
them his laws and instructions.'*

'This is not good!' His father-in-law exclaimed.

*'You're going to wear yourself out-and the people,
too. This job is too heavy a burden for you to handle all
by yourself.'*

Exodus 18:1 tells us that Jethro is a pastor in the
city of Midian. I think it is important to understand that
Jethro is a spiritual leader in the life of Moses. Moses has
found himself in a very hard place—he is about to be
overcome by life's challenges. Moses is about to fail. If
you're like me about now, you're starting to wonder,
"How is it possible that Moses, of all people, is about to
fail?" The man who seemed like nothing could ever be
too hard! It was not too hard for him to face Pharaoh. It
was not too hard for him to lead a million plus people out
of bondage—bondage that had lasted for four hundred
years! It was not too hard for him to trust God when it
was time to cross the Red Sea. It seemed that nothing was
too hard for this man. Then one day, he hit a hard place.
I call this the Law of Hard.

> **My definition of The Law of Hard:**
> **Whatever you find hard in life has the potential
> to define your life, your business, and your min-
> istry, temporarily and/or permanently.**

40

If your marriage becomes too hard for you, then you will be defined as a divorcée (or divorcé). If drinking a glass of wine with your meal becomes too hard for you, then you will be defined as an alcoholic. The Law of Hard affects every area of our life.

Moses found himself at the point of failure. The truth is that every person at one time or another in his or her life will hit a hard place, which could become a point of potential failure. If something didn't change quickly in the life of Moses, then he would have failed. But Jethro, a spiritual leader, spoke wisdom and strategy into the life of Moses.

Exodus 18:23-26 (NLT)

*'If you follow this advice, **and** if God directs you to do so, **then** you will be able to endure the pressures, and all these people will go home in peace.'*

Moses listened to his father-in-law's advice and followed his suggestions.

He chose capable men from all over Israel and made them judges over the people. They were put in charge of groups of one thousand, one hundred, fifty, and ten.

*These men were constantly available to administer justice. They brought the **hard cases** to Moses, but they judged the smaller matters themselves.*

The challenges of a growing ministry became too hard for Moses. But just in time, a spiritual leader named Jethro arrived on the scene. Jethro noticed right away that Moses was facing challenges that had the potential to overcome him. In verse 17, Jethro tells Moses, "The thing you do is not good!" Can I tell you the truth today? We all need spiritual leadership that has the ability and permission to look into our life and tell us if they see anything in us that is not good! Now I'm not saying that you should blindly follow a man or a woman and forget about God. I'm saying that the two work together—they are designed to work hand in hand.

In verse 23 we find the formula for success. Jethro tells Moses, "If you will listen to my advice and if God commands you then you will have success." I want you to understand the pattern, *IF, AND, & THEN.* First, Jethro is giving Moses wisdom and strategy to help him overcome a life and ministry challenge. Notice the little but powerful word *if.* Jethro tells Moses, "I am giving you some good advice, and if you will listen to the wisdom in my advice, then I believe you will see success." But Jethro doesn't stop there. He continues by saying that Moses should take this wisdom and strategy to God and if God says yes, then he will see true success in his life.

One day, while our family was living in Wales, we received a call from our pastor, Kevin Gerald. Pastor Kevin told us that whenever he thought about or prayed for our family he had the thought, "Suggest to Eddie and Tammy that they should come back to America for two to six months." When he told me this, at first I thought he was playing around. He quickly let me know that he was not teasing. I then asked him if there was anything he was not telling me. He said no that was all he knew. He asked me what it would take for us to come home. I told him four plane tickets, and I would need to cancel twenty to sixty churches that had scheduled us for ministry. Many of these churches had been waiting for almost one year for a date for us to come. Pastor Kevin then told us to think and to pray about it. Whatever we decided, it was OK with him. Seven days later, we were on a plane for

America. Over a two-year period of time my wife, Tammy, had gone to her doctor several times in the United Kingdom. She had four moles that were causing us great concern. Each time she had them checked, her doctor told her that there was no need to worry.

While we were on the airplane back to America, one of the moles got bumped and bled on Tammy's blouse. When we arrived in Seattle, Tammy decided that she would go to her family doctor in America. Two days later, as the doctor looked at the moles, he had immediate concern. He removed all four of the moles that day and had them sent to the lab. When the tests came back two days later, we were told two of the moles had cancer in them. The doctor told us that he removed them all successfully, and now there was nothing to worry about. But if they had not been taken off, eventually, it could have cost Tammy her life. Within two months, we were back in the United Kingdom, and we carried on with the ministry there.

As you read this story, did you hear the Jethro Formula? Our pastor called us in the country of Wales with advice, wisdom, and strategy. He then said, "Get with God and pray about it. And *if* you feel that God is in this wisdom and strategy, *and* He instructs you to come home, *then* you will have success!"

The Law of Hard affects every one of our lives! But more importantly it affects our Personal Capacity!

CHAPTER 7

THE HARD THRESHOLD

Over the past five years, my wife, Tammy, and I have traveled full time. We have had the privilege of ministering in hundreds of churches around the world. But to tell you the truth, there have been many times I have scratched my head and said, "God, what is going on here?" An example would be, why do some churches grow and others do not grow? There are churches that have a great pastor with an evident call on their life, with great vision, great location, great passion and great worship, but they don't grow. Then I have watched other churches that don't seem to have as much going for them, their vision is unclear and not communicated well. Their church is in a bad location, no parking, sometimes the music is painful to listen to, but they just keep growing.

If you're like me, you have known individuals who seem to be so talented, so capable, so qualified, and have such a large Personal Capacity, but yet they never rise to a level of effectiveness that matches their ability and/or gifting. And then there are other people who don't seem to have as much ability, talent, and gifting, but it never seems to stop them from rising in the leadership journey.

I have watched hundreds of leaders over the past few years looking for answers. I have begun to see a common thread that runs throughout all people in leadership. Some people have the talent and technical skills needed for a specific task and position, but because of a Low Threshold of Hard they fall short of their personal potential.

Diagram #1

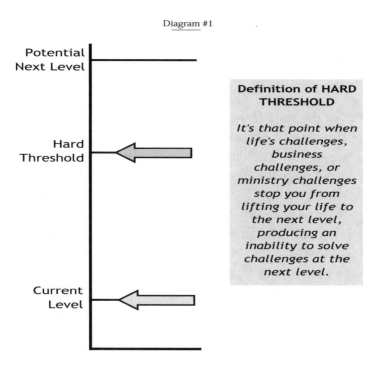

Potential
Next Level

Hard
Threshold

Current
Level

Definition of HARD THRESHOLD

It's that point when life's challenges, business challenges, or ministry challenges stop you from lifting your life to the next level, producing an inability to solve challenges at the next level.

Why is our Threshold of Hard so important? It has the potential of becoming our Failing Point. When a person continually runs over and over again into their Hard Threshold and cannot seem to lift their life above that level, it will ultimately become the Failing Point in their life.

I am asked all the time, "How do you know the level of your Hard Threshold?" The answer is simply that you don't know exactly where your Hard Threshold is until you reach it. But there are indicators that alert you as you approach your Hard Threshold.

Diagram #2

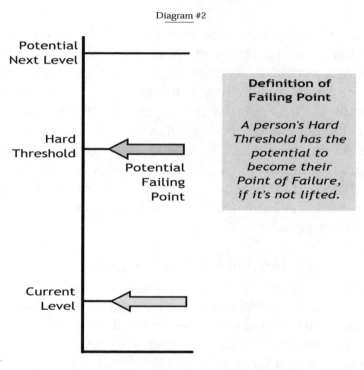

Threshold of Hard for Individuals

Let me give you a few of the indicators that tell us when a person is approaching the Hard Threshold in their life. I call this the Compression of Hard! One of the first indicators is pressure in your relationships. It is hard to really figure out exactly what is wrong with the relationship, but something is wrong. More and more misunderstandings begin to happen, you seem to have a lack of patience in the relationship, and frustration builds. You begin to have mounting pressure on the job. Your workload becomes overwhelming, and you begin to have a hard time focusing on the task at hand.

A person's Hard Threshold has the potential to become their Point of Failure if it's not lifted.

There is an increase of tension in your work environment and the family environment. This is the point where a person starts planning their escape! They start daydreaming about a new marriage, a new job, or a new church. At this point, a person can become physically sick. I'm not talking about an imaginary sickness because the condition is real. I'm talking about conditions like migraines, depression, and anxiety attacks. But the origin of this condition is not physical; it is caused by the increasing pressure felt as a person approaches their Hard Threshold.

Threshold of Hard for Teams

When a team's problems become too hard to solve based on their current skill and competency, it will hold them at that same level; thus creating the potential for a Reoccurring problem. There are two kinds of Reoccurring problems: Same-Level Reoccurring Problems and Next-Level Reoccurring Problems.

A team's Hard Threshold is a direct result of their Same-Level Reoccurring Problems.

Let me give you a few of the indicators that tell us when a team is approaching their Hard Threshold. First, the team experiences an increase of Same-Level Reoccurring Problems. As the Compression of Hard increases, the team's frustration factor builds as a result of the increase of Reoccurring problems. The team now experiences an increased pressure among members. The team begins to lose sight of their objectives while focusing more and more on personal issues. Finally, battle lines are formed around personal issues. Our team has arrived at the Failing Point. Now they begin to plan their escape!

Diagram #3

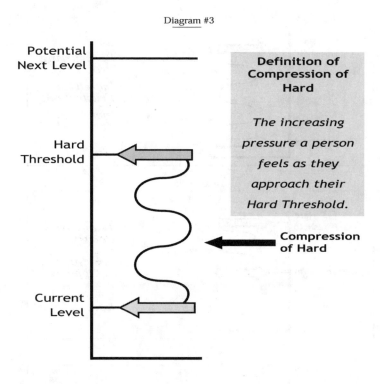

We will all, at one time or another, find ourselves at the Failing Point. What you do there will shape your future!

Every person has a Threshold of Hard. For many people, this threshold is moveable. It can be lifted! When champions find themselves in a hard place, they don't run. Instead, they stand and hold steady under the pressure. They will be able to lift and move the Level of Hard in their life. Sometimes it's thinking that must change. Sometimes more education lifts our threshold. In my ministry, my new office equipment lifted my Hard Threshold and moved us from a place of incompetence to a place of competence.

Diagram #4

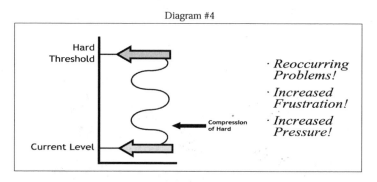

· *Reoccurring Problems!*

· *Increased Frustration!*

· *Increased Pressure!*

Diagram #5

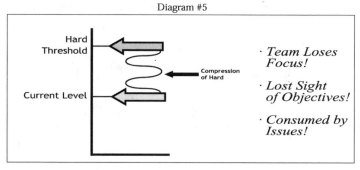

· *Team Loses Focus!*

· *Lost Sight of Objectives!*

· *Consumed by Issues!*

Diagram #6

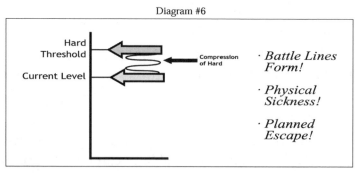

· *Battle Lines Form!*

· *Physical Sickness!*

· *Planned Escape!*

For others, their threshold has become seemingly unmovable. Why? Because of embedded thinking patterns and a compilation of life's experiences and tradition. An inability to lift your Hard Threshold will produce a pressure that makes most people want to plan their escape! The increasing compression drives you into your Hard Threshold.

Far too many people have their thinking set firmly in past experiences and traditionalism.

Let's look at four areas that will help us lift our Hard Threshold.

(1) Thinking patterns

A person's thinking is like a set of railroad tracks. We had better know what train we are on! Earlier this year, Tammy and I were in London, and we had decided to go to Paris on the Euro Star train. As we walked into the Waterloo train station, I noticed that there were dozens of train tracks leaving the station all heading in the same direction. No one would think that they made dozens of tracks all going to Paris. We know that at some point the tracks will split away from each other and lead to many numerous destinations. Some will go to Wales, others to Scotland, and one of those tracks goes to Paris, France. We had to make sure that the train we got on was going to Paris. Not just any train would get us there. If we got on the wrong train we could end up in Ireland, Amsterdam, or many other destinations.

Your thinking works in much the same way. You had better know what train of thought you are on because that train is taking you somewhere! Every one of your thoughts may leave the station seemingly headed in the same direction, but know that at some point, that thought may take you to a place you never intended to go! I have had so many people tell me, "It was just a harmless thought!" But that first harmless thought became the first thought in a long line of thoughts that took this person to a destination they never intended to go.

A person who is serious about lifting their Hard Threshold has embraced a thinking pattern that eagerly accepts change when challenged by their leader, or a sense of God directing them somewhere new.

It was a very warm August afternoon when I had been speaking at a friend's church in the L.A. area. I was very tired, but at the same time, excited to be on my way home to be with my family. As I stood in line ready to board my flight from Ontario, California, to Seattle, Washington, I heard a lot of commotion behind me at the airport security area. A man covered in sweat came running down the airport terminal, bumping into several people. He ran straight to the front of the line I was standing in, waiting to board the plane. Completely out of breath the man said to the ticket agent, "I am late for an appointment in Seattle. I need to board the plane immediately!" he commanded. He became very upset when the ticket agent told him he would need to take his place at the end of the line. She said, "Sir, it does not matter if you're the first one on the plane or the last one on the plane, we will all arrive in Seattle at the same time!"

You should have seen the look on his face. The next few words out of his mouth were classic. As he walked to the back of the line he said, "I don't know what I was thinking!" His unreasonable behavior started with a single thought! A "train of thoughts" took form, and it led him to a destination he never intended to go. Once he stopped long enough to hear what the gate attendant said, he realized how silly his thinking was. We must take a good look and ask ourselves if the thinking we currently have will get us to the place we really want to go in life. If we discover that the train of thinking we are on is leading us in the wrong direction, then we have to be responsible enough and mature enough to change it.

(2) The size of the challenges

I know so many talented leaders, leaders that have what I call Breakout Potential. Their creativity, their education, and their potential to succeed are second to none. If you had to pick someone out of a crowd that you thought had the potential to do something significant, then you would pick them out. So many times, I have watched people like them become overwhelmed by average-sized challenges.

Having high levels of training and technical skill do not always guarantee success. I have been amazed how an average-sized challenge can stop even a high-capacity person.

A person's success in life will be affected by the size of challenges that stop them.

I remember reading that a space shuttle launch was canceled because of a relatively inexpensive mechanical part. Think about it, a space launch costing millions of dollars was canceled because of a small little part that malfunctioned. Millions of dollars spent on an incredible project stopped by the failure of an item that cost only a few cents.

(3) The size of the Reoccurring Problems we solve

The truth is that a person will never stop having challenges! There is no way to stop them, but we can stop many Reoccurring Problems.

There are two kinds of Reoccurring Problems.

- *Reoccurring Problems we can do nothing about.*
- *Reoccurring Problems we can do something about.*

There are also two levels of Reoccurring Problems:

- *Next-Level* **Reoccurring Problems!**
- *Same-Level* **Reoccurring Problems!**

First, let's look at Reoccurring Problems that we can do nothing about. The weather would be an example of a Reoccurring Problem a person can do nothing about. Let's say a person lives in Minnesota. Every year, we know that there will be several snowstorms that will affect the normal operations of our business, which will in turn affect our organization's finances. We don't know how many storms will come and how often they will come through our city. This is a Reoccurring Problem we can do nothing about.

Power outages could be a Reoccurring Problem. Let's say there is a two-year revitalization project in our section of the city. The power can and does go off when we least expect it. This is a Reoccurring Problem we can do little if anything about.

Now let's look at Reoccurring Problems we can do something about. For example, I will use the sound and media department of an organization. Let's say a speaker walks onto the platform to address the audience, and the microphone is not turned up on time or squeals with feedback. If this occurs once or twice a year, it is understandable because of many factors that could be affecting the sound system at that moment. But, if it happens more than once, and it just so happens that the problem occurs when the same sound tech is working the controls, you have the potential of experiencing a Reoccurring Problem. Most of the time, this is caused from a lack of focus by the sound person or a lack of training.

Tardiness is another example of a Reoccurring Problem. If a person is chronically late for work and appointments, then it is obviously a Reoccurring Problem in the person's life. It honestly does not matter how skilled this person is on the job, if they can't get to work on time then they eventually would be fired! Even small Reoccurring Problems in our life can cause us big problems. A person will not rise above the level of Reoccurring Problems in their life.

There are two kinds of Reoccurring Problems that affect us. Problems we can do nothing about and problems we can do something about. Now we will look at two levels of Reoccurring Problems. Reoccurring Problems are like a person going round and around the mountain. It is OK to go

> **If a problem is too hard for that person based on the person's current skill and competency level, then it creates the potential for a Reoccurring Problem.**

around the mountain as long as we are gaining some kind of altitude! Naturally, there are some problems that will be waiting for us at each new level. I call them Next-Level

Reoccurring Problems. An example for your organization might be cash flow. Another example might be car parking. These are examples of Reoccurring Problems waiting for an organization at each new level of growth. There is no way to get away from Next-Level Reoccurring Problems.

The problems start with Same-Level Reoccurring Problems that cannot be overcome. When a person or organization faces the same level of problems over and over again and cannot find a way to overcome it, they have found their Hard Threshold. Given enough time, this Hard Threshold has the *potential* to become our Failing Point. Hence the saying, "Here today gone tomorrow."

If a problem is not properly diagnosed, then it will not be properly solved; thus creating the potential for a Reoccurring Problem.

What is the cause of Reoccurring Problems? If a problem is not properly diagnosed, then it will not be properly solved; thus creating the potential for the Reoccurring Problem to happen again and again.

A second cause of a Reoccurring Problem could be that the problem is too *hard* for that person based the person's current skill and competency level. This will hold them at their current level or push them into incompetence, which ultimately will become their Failing Point. Not having an adequate skill and competency level will create the potential for a Reoccurring Problem and failure.

(4) The ability to stand under pressure

At what level and amount of pressure can a person stand before retreating or collapsing? I have known people that always run when they start to feel an uncomfortable amount of pressure in their lives. They run from their marriage only to arrive at the same point in the next marriage, and then they run again. They run from their job, their church, and their relationships just to find themselves back in the same position or similar condition in their new job, their new church, and their new relationships. I have a friend that has this problem. When they are facing challenges in their relationships, they always get physically sick. They have several days of headaches, and they miss work. The truth is that they are hiding. I don't believe for one minute that they are faking the way they are feeling. It is just that they become so overwhelmed mentally that it affects them physically.

Let me give you a couple of ways to increase the amount of pressure you can stand. First, I make my top ten challenges line up and take a number. No matter how loud they are yelling in my head, I make them shut up and wait their turn. Now I make them line up from the most important to least important. You cannot effectively tackle ten challenges at once. Once you have them lined up, pick one challenge you can do something about. So many people make themselves sick worrying about challenges they can do little, if anything, about.

You must understand worry is the enemy of faith. Worry has never helped a person solve a single challenge. The truth is that worry delays their ability to solve the challenge. So a person must clear their mind of all the millions of negative thoughts that are flooding in. First, they must free their mind from worry. Secondly, they must pick one challenge to work on.

My son Daniel is nineteen years old. A few months ago, he decided to start working out. He was watching a guy in the gym doing dozens of handstand pushups. When Daniel tried to do them, he could only do one. When he tried to do a second one, he failed — it was too much weight. His Hard Threshold was one handstand pushup! At that point, Daniel had a decision to make. Was he going to be satisfied with only being able to do one handstand pushup while other guys could do dozens? Daniel started exercising three times per week. After three months, Daniel can now do over twenty-five handstand pushups at a time. He had lifted his Hard Threshold twenty-five times higher.

In this chapter you have seen the effects of the Threshold of Hard in a person's life. It is essential that you keep lifting your Hard Threshold, always moving forward in life! You cannot let pressure, challenges, reoccurring problems, or small thinking stop you from growing and going to the next level in your life. Lifting your Hard Threshold starts by understanding that it exists and it must be lifted. As you read further through the pages of this book you will receive powerful insights for lifting your Hard Threshold.

CHAPTER 8

CAPACITY INDICATORS: GOD'S PLACE OF FAVOR

**To increase my Personal Capacity,
I must find God's place of favor for my life!**

What does the favor of God look like? I have asked hundreds of people that question. And the majority of the time people never describe to me what the favor of God looks like in their own personal life. They describe to me what they think the favor of God looks like in other people's lives.

Psalm 89:17 (NLT)

"You are their glorious strength. Our power is based on your favor."

Psalm 86:17 (NLT)

"Send me a sign of your favor."

On a Sunday morning, while living in High Wycombe, England, my family got in the car and started down the motorway. This was a normal Sunday for us. Get up early and drive for several hours to minister in church. While driving to my destination, I remember thinking to myself, "We are making great time this morning."

Then I heard my daughter, Bethany's voice, "Daddy, where are we going today?"

I said, "We are going to preach in South Wales today, baby." Everything was going so good that morning, and there was very little traffic.

Then a few minutes later Bethany made another statement, "Daddy, I don't remember this being the way to Wales."

I said, "Baby, you just relax and leave the driving to Daddy!"

A few minutes later, Bethany asked me the question, "Why are there no road signs that say South Wales, Daddy?" Then she said, "All the road signs say 'Oxford.' Daddy, isn't Oxford in the wrong direction?"

Tammy had been resting with her eyes closed, but I remember at that moment she opened one eye, smiled, and said, "That's my girl." All I remember is that I was making great time going in the wrong direction. To finish the story, I turned around and started following the signs to South Wales. We barely made it to church in time to preach that day.

The highway department puts out signs to let you know that you are going in the right direction, and so does God! It is called His FAVOR!

When I looked through the Bible to see what the favor of God looked like, I began to discover that the favor of God looked different in every single person I read about. I could not find any two people in whom the favor of God looked exactly the same!

I know many people who seem to be making great time in life, but I wonder if they are going in the wrong direction. Why do I say this? I say this because there are no signs of His favor in their life. If you don't discover what the favor of God looks like in your own personal life, then you will become disillusioned, you'll lose hope, and you'll become jealous, or

> **The favor of God does not look the same on any two people.**

envious when you see the favor of God in other people's lives. Far too many people are not reaching their personal potential in life, and I believe one reason is because they have not found God's place of favor for their life!

I grew up in a pastor's home, so I was always around ministers. I was like the fly on the wall. I got to hang around so many great ministers. I listened to what seemed like thousands of conversations and stories about all the awesome things God had done and was doing. But I must tell you that the prophets were my favorite. I would sit in church and watch and listen to them in awe. I thought to myself many times that if I get to choose what gift I have, I want to be a prophet. When I got a little older and started in ministry, I really desired to prophesy over people. Plus the Bible says, "desire the best gifts." As far as I was concerned, that would be to prophesy.

Just like every person has a different set of finger-prints, a different DNA code, so does every person have their own place of favor in God!

It has been over twenty-two years since I started in ministry. But to tell you the truth, there was a hidden struggle going on inside me. No one knew about it for the most part. Well, my dad knew something, I think. He would say, "Son, you cannot walk in another man's anointing." I don't know if it was the way my dad tried to explain it to me or that the timing wasn't right, but I just didn't get it. I experienced many years of inner frustration, self-questioning. Why was God not letting me do what was in my heart to do? All I wanted to do was prophesy.

It was a beautiful Saturday morning in the United Kingdom. Five pastors had asked Tammy and I to mentor them, so we had them over to our house. We had a great time with them, and it turned out to be a great benefit to them. Over the next several months, over one hundred more pastors asked us to give them mentoring — modeling principles for their personal life and ministry. Over the next year, it doubled again and is still growing.

Can you guess when I really began to see true success in our ministry? When I quit going in a direction that had no signs of God's favor. I have now learned to flow towards the signs of God's favor in my life.

I have had several friends say to me, "How is it possible that the rancher, Eddie Windsor, has so many pastors around the world wanting him to mentor them?" They say, "I just don't get it."

I had a very large American ministry call me while I was in the United Kingdom. They said, "We have been trying to establish our ministry in the UK for several years with little or no success." When they told me how much money they were investing each year in their UK efforts, I realized it was more than I had made in five or more years. They said to me, "We just don't get it. How can you accomplish so much in such a short amount of time without enough money, and you don't even have a known name?"

I simply replied to them the only possible answer, "It's called the favor of God."

God's favor is on the fruit of my life!

I flow towards the favor of God in my life. God's favor is on the fruit of my life. I'm not suggesting you only follow signs, but I have found that the signs of God's favor tell me I'm going in the right direction.

God spoke to my wife's heart one day after just moving to the United Kingdom. He said, "I never said that it would be easy, I only said that it was possible!" Things may not be easy, but it doesn't mean that it's not God's plan for your life. But, just like the highway department has a sign every so often along the motorway, you should be seeing some kind of a sign of God's favor in your life along the way. Just make sure that you're not making good time going in the wrong direction in your life.

CAPACITY INDICATORS:
THE GIFT THAT SERVES BEST

**To increase my Personal Capacity
I must find the *gift* in me that *BEST SERVES*!**

1 Peter 4:10 tells us that, "as each one of you have received a gift, minister that gift to one another." Every person has been given gifts that God placed in our lives for a purpose.

Would you agree with me today in saying that the church was God's idea? The Bible is very clear that the church was God's idea! I have said many times, "I wish the church would have been my idea," because the church was a great idea. Would you agree with me today in saying that God has placed the responsibility for the stewardship of the church in the local pastor's hands? I think we all agree on that point. Someone must be responsible, and God has clearly assigned the local pastor that responsibility.

Sometimes when I finish speaking, people come up to me and say, "Eddie you are so anointed!" or "You have such a gift!" Can I share with you a key that I've learned about the gifts God placed within me? When I put the gifts in me to work in my local church and when I place my gifts in the hands of my pastor, I believe my gifts or the call of God on my life becomes more effective. It is able to accomplish more, it lifts more people, it encourages more people, and it blesses more people!

I believe that the apostle, prophet, evangelist, and teacher are at their best when they work hand in hand with the local church and the local pastor. But I also believe that the gifts God has placed in each one of our lives become more effective when we put them to work in our church, serving alongside our local pastor.

You might be thinking, "Eddie, I attend a very large church. My pastor doesn't even know who I am! I have only spoken to him personally a couple of times. I'm sure he's not aware of my gifts, or that I even have any. I would feel fairly sure that he doesn't even know my name!" What you're saying is probably accurate. But do you want to know the good news? Your pastor doesn't have to know your name. He might not be aware of your individual gifts, or a specific gift you have, but believe me, he is aware you have a gift. I can say that because your pastor knows what the Bible says, and the Bible says in 1 Peter 4:10, "…that each person has received a gift from God!"

**Of the many gifts in you, which best serve
your pastor, your church, and the Kingdom of God?**

That is the number one key to the many gifts in you. It's not about which gift or gifts you like to serve with. Far too many people are telling God what they will or will not do for Him! Most people pick out the gift they want to serve with and then try to force it on their church. The big question for you today is, of the many gifts in you,

> **To increase your Personal Capacity you must find your gift that best serves!**

which gifts best serve your local church? You may sing better than any person that sings on the platform at your church. However, you must understand that if your singing gift is not what your church needs from you, then that is not the gift that best serves.

I'm sure you now have several questions to ask me like, "What do I do first?" I would start by listening. Each week, when your pastor and leaders stand before the church, they inform you of places within the church where you can use your gifts. During the announcements, they will make you aware of many opportunities. When your pastor preaches, he will mention things in the ministry that need volunteers.

The second thing I suggest is to experiment. Volunteer for an event to help out with the children or youth. I started out by volunteering in the junior high classroom. Over a fifteen-year time frame, I did just about everything in my local church. I worked with children, helped out with church cleaning, helped on the construction of the church addition, served as the youth pastor, preached for the pastor when he was out of town, administration and much more. I would simply listen, volunteer, and experience.

I think it is time for a story from my life. I was raised in the country on our family's cattle ranch. Six weeks after Tammy and I got married, we started volunteering in our church. We started out working with junior high kids. After several years of volunteering in just about every department in the church, the pastor asked me to preach for him from time to time. One Sunday morning, I was all ready to preach. I had my best suit on. I had spent more hours than you can imagine in preparation getting ready to preach this message. The service had started, and I had made my way to the front row of the church. We had just started the second worship song, when I felt a tap on my shoulder. I turned to see one of the ushers looking at me—he had that bad kind of look in his eyes. He then proceeded to tell me that none of the toilets in the building were working. The toilets in the basement had started to overflow.

Instantly, I thought about the potential problem of having several hundred people in a country church where the next public toilets were about three miles away. I quickly thought about possible options. I knew what the problem most likely was. It was something in our septic pump system that had quit working. I had fixed it once before when it had done this same thing several years earlier.

Then the real fear hit me when I realized I was the only one that knew how to fix the problem during the service, and I was also going to be speaking in about fifteen minutes. I turned to my wife, and said, "I'll be back!" And out the back of the church I went with five ushers. As we were walking around behind the building, I was taking off my suit jacket and tucking my tie into my shirt. We took the lid off the septic pump chamber. Two big ushers held my arms as I leaned down into the tank. It was just as I thought—a wire nut had come loose over time. I temporarily tightened the nut. I yelled to the third usher, standing at the back of the building and holding the emergency shut off, "Turn it on!" The pump started up! Up they pulled me! A fourth usher had wet towels to clean my hands. They had some cologne they sprayed on me, and we entered the service just as they were finishing the announcements.

Within a couple of minutes I was up preaching. After the service, so many people said they had never heard me speak so well. They said, "It was a whole new level of ministry for you." They used words like, "The anointing was the strongest we have ever seen it," but I knew it was because I had used the gifts in me that best served that day!

I understand that at any given moment I must be ready to find the gift in me that will best serve my pastor, my church, and that will ultimately best serve the Kingdom of God!

You could be sitting in a great church week after week and personally be going through a forty-year wilderness experience. But you could be sitting right next to someone else that has entered into their promised land because they have found the gift in them that best serves.

Today, the real question for you is, "Of the many gifts in you, which gifts do you have that will best serve your local church?" There are many things Tammy and I could do for our Pastors Kevin and Sheila Gerald at Covenant Celebration Church. I could be an usher or Tammy could sing in the choir. But we have discovered the gifts in us that best serve our pastor, our home church, and the Kingdom of God are the ones we use when we get on an airplane to the United Kingdom, work with pastors, and build churches there.

I cannot encourage you enough to place your gifts in the hands of your church's vision and see God use your gifts the way they were intended to be used! When we find those gifts in us that best serve, they become indicators pointing us in the direction of our Personal Capacity!

CAPACITY ACCELERATOR: AN OPEN HAND

To increase my Personal Capacity, I must hold my position with an OPEN HAND!

We have already established today that God has placed the responsibility for the stewardship of the church in the local pastor's hands.

One morning, when I was about six or seven years old, my dad came into my bedroom and said, "Son let's go for a walk." I mentioned to you earlier that I was raised on a cattle ranch with hundreds of acres of land. It was a warm summer morning as we walked across the fields together. My dad began to talk to me about God's call on my life. I really didn't understand what it meant that day, but I listened to every word.

He said, "Son you have many great gifts that God has placed in you. But, son, you must understand you don't own the gifts in you—God does. He owns the gifts in you, but He has made you a steward of those gifts. It is your responsibility to develop the gifts and apply proper stewardship to them. Son, if you will develop the gifts in you, then they will create opportunities and positions for you. Always remember to hold your opportunities and positions with an open hand, and God will do significant things through your life." My dad told me this for what felt like hundreds of times in my life. Keep an open hand!

We do not own the gift in us, God does!
He has just made us a steward of His property!

When I was about sixteen years old, I went to my pastor and asked if there was something I could do to help in the ministry or around the church property.

He asked me to help out on the construction crew of the new building. We were building a new church sanctuary at the time so my first job in the ministry was being a helper on the church building's construction crew. After about two years, the building was done, so I went back to my pastor and asked for something more to do. This time, he asked me to work with junior high kids in the ministry.

Let me illustrate it like this. Each time my pastor asked me to do something in the church, it was like putting a cup of water into my open hand. Then each time when I finished the job, or he was ready to have me do something else, it was like taking the cup back and placing a different cup into my open hand!

After a year or so, my pastor asked me if I would teach in Sunday school. Then he asked me to take care of the facilities. Who better then me—I knew that building inside and out! Then I became a youth worker and janitor together. Then I became the youth pastor. After a while, I became an associate pastor. It was like going back and forth to the pastor, and with each new position, he would take the previous cup and place a new cup into my open hand. I had a wonderful relationship with my pastor because my father taught me at a very young age that I did not own the gifts in me. God did! God has just made me a steward of His property, and He owns the gifts in us!

Proverbs 18:16

"A man's gift makes room for him, And brings him before great men."

Over a fifteen-year time period, I held numerous positions in that church. Most people find it easy to hold their position with an open hand if they really don't like the job they have been given. When pastor called me into his office and said that he was going to have someone else do the janitorial work, I found it very easy to hold my hand out so he could take that position and give it to someone else. The problem arises when we like what we are doing.

It becomes harder and harder to hold your position with an open hand if your self-worth and your identity become intertwined in the position!

I have noticed that a person's language and termi-nology changes as well. At one time, they would have said, "This particular ministry position is where I 'serve' in the church." Now they are saying things like, "My ministry, my calling! Have you seen the level of anointing on me lately? No, don't touch me we'll both go down!" Their ministry theme song becomes, "I exalt me, I exalt me, I exalt me O Lord!"

1 Samuel 15:17

"So Samuel said, 'When you were little in your own eyes, were you not head of the tribes of Israel? And did not the Lord anoint you king over Israel?'"

Saul, like so many, started with the right intentions, but he lost focus along the way. The life of Saul is one of lost potential. Just think about it, the King of the Children of Israel. All he had to do was keep his heart right and his head small.

Romans 12:3 (Today's English Version)

"Do not think of yourself more highly than you should. Instead, be modest in your thinking and judge yourself according to the amount of faith that God has given you."

1 Samuel 15:19

"Samuel said to Saul, 'Why then did you not obey the voice of the Lord?'"

Samuel had the responsibility of confronting Saul for his misuse of position in the Kingdom of God. Can you guess what needs to happen when you have someone in a ministry position that is holding on for all they're worth? Our self-worth comes from knowing who we are in God, but far too often a person tries to get their self-worth and their identity from their position. Often, it seems as if they personally cease to exist. Now it's all about the gift and the position. Next, they become very controlling with their position. So a senior pastor knows he is responsible before God to confront this person that is out of control. So he reaches for the position that you are holding in your hand. But instead of holding the position with an open hand, you pull back from the pastor crushing the cup! Water goes everywhere!

At this point, what normally happens is, everything is blamed on the pastor, and you leave the church. So you go to another church in town, and within a short period of time, the pastor there says, "You have a gift!" He notices that you have a few holes and cracks in your cup. You tell him how "that pastor" across town hurt you and your gift. So he decides that he will personally pour himself into helping you, but as he pours into you, his efforts—the water—run out onto the floor. You decide that he cannot help you, so you go to another church and another church and another church.

Often when a person first gets involved in the ministry, they say, "Pastor just use me." But after a while they started saying, "Pastor is just using me!"

It does not matter how much or how fast you pour the water into this leaky vessel, eventually it runs out. I have seen people go through this cycle over and over again in church after church, watching pastor after pastor pour into leaky vessels. You can go to God to get your gift fixed. Get your life fixed. But it will happen again if you don't understand that you must hold the position you have been placed in with an open hand! I am not saying that there is not the potential of being hurt. There is always the potential of being misused. I can tell you from personal experience.

A person who decides not to allow another person's actions or reactions to dictate their actions or reactions, experiences an empowering freedom.

If you want to increase your Personal Capacity, then you must recognize that your emotional reactions are your own personal responsibility. You must decide not to allow another person's actions to dictate your actions or reactions. You will never increase your capacity as long as you allow yourself the privilege of playing the blame game.

A free person is master of himself. If you want to experience an empowering freedom, then stop playing the blame game and start taking responsibility for all your actions. The sooner you realize no one can choose your reactions but you, the sooner you will have the benefits of an increased capacity.

Holding your gift with an open hand starts with trusting God! Know that He holds the hearts of His shepherds in His hand.

1 Peter 5:2-4 (KJV)

Feed the flock of God which is among you, taking the oversight thereof, not by constraint, but willingly; not for filthy lucre, but of a ready mind;
Neither as being lords over God's heritage, but being examples to the flock.
And when the chief Shepherd shall appear, ye shall receive a crown of glory that fadeth not away.

CHAPTER 11

CAPACITY ACCELERATOR:
THE RIGHT SACRIFICES

**To increase my Personal Capacity,
I must make the RIGHT SACRIFICES.**

If you're going to increase your Personal Capacity, you must make the right sacrifices in life.

Psalm 4:5 (NIV)

"Offer right sacrifices and trust in the Lord."

I guess one of the most important lessons I have learned is that life is full of sacrifice. One day in London, I was sitting in a workshop, listening to Dr. Jim Reeve teach a group of church leaders. I remember the exact moment when he quoted Psalm 4:5 and said, "You will never escape making sacrifices in life!" I can honestly say that his words changed my life that day. Just because you are making sacrifices does not guarantee you've made the right sacrifice!

There are *right sacrifices*, and there are *wrong sacrifices* in this life!

Malachi 1:8 (NLT)

"When you give blind animals as sacrifices, isn't that wrong?"

Philippians 4:18

I am full, having received from Epaphroditus the things sent from you, a sweet-smelling aroma, an acceptable sacrifice, well pleasing to God.
And my God shall supply all your need according to His riches in glory by Christ Jesus.

Many of us are paying the high cost of sacrifice, trying to please people, but it's not working. You might decide to move to Zimbabwe to be a missionary. Make a great sacrifice in moving your family and leaving your church, your job! But if God is not asking you to move there, then it is the wrong sacrifice. Often a man will work long hours trying to get financial gain to provide a certain level of lifestyle for his wife and family. In his mind, he is giving up many things that he would like to be doing, but he gladly gives his time thinking it will be best for his family's future. When he arrives in his future, his children don't have time for him because they don't have a relationship, and his wife wants a divorce. The next words out of his mouth have been spoken millions of times by men around the globe. "I have worked my fingers to the bone. I have sacrificed all my desires for my wife, and now, she's leaving me!"

The truth is he did sacrifice a lot, but most of the time, it was the wrong sacrifice. What was a sacrifice to him was a point of contention for her. She wanted quality time with her husband and family. He didn't have time to spend with the family because he was sacrificing all his time for the family making ends meet.

If I want to sacrifice my time for my wife, it would be through an act of service—my wife's love language. If she sees me making sacrifices in those areas, it is meaningful to her. Now my daughter, Bethany, is different. It would be quality time for her. That's what she wants from her daddy! When I come home from a long ministry road trip, I don't need to bring my girl a gift. But what I do need to do is schedule about two or three hours of hanging out with her. Tucking her into bed at night and talking with her about her day. And my son is different again. Life is all about making the right choices and making the right sacrifices. To tell you the truth, there is nothing I wouldn't do for my family. No price is too great! But if I'm going to make a great sacrifice, I need to make sure I am speaking the right language. A language that is understood and meaningful to the people I love!

A man might say, "I do appreciate my wife keeping the house clean. But, honestly, I would rather have the house less tidy if that would help my wife not to be so tired at the end of the day so we could spend some intimate time together." He might say, "She works so hard keeping our home in perfect condition." The meals are five course meals every night, but by the time we get ready for bed, she is exhausted and falls to sleep. Her motive for working so hard on their home and meals is to be a great wife and please her husband, but she is speaking the wrong language. She is making the wrong sacrifice that is costing her more than she thinks.

1 Samuel 15:22

And Samuel said, 'Has the Lord as great a delight in burnt offerings and sacrifices, as in obeying the voice of the LORD? Behold, to obey is better than sacrifice, and to listen than the fat of rams.'

Truthfully, when I started making the right sacrifices, I felt my capacity increase. No longer did it feel like I was spinning my wheels going nowhere. As a husband, I know my wife is pleased with the hard work and sacrifice I am making. As a father, I know my children are pleased and fulfilled by the effort and sacrifice I make for them. As a son of God, when I know my Father in heaven is pleased with my sacrifice, I feel like no amount of effort is too great! No sacrifice is too great or too small when it is the right one.

> **There are right sacrifices and there are wrong sacrifices in life!**

CHAPTER
12

CAPACITY INCREASER: PERSONAL GROWTH PLAN

**To increase my Personal Capacity, I
must have a Personal Growth Plan.**

L et me give you an example of how promotion works in
most churches and many businesses today. First, they
find a person who is available and willing. Bingo, they've
got the job. Most organizations are so excited to have volunteers they will take any warm, breathing body. So if this
person stays faithful, we promote them. If they stay faithful, we promote them again. If they continue to come to
work, and they don't steal money, then we promote them
again. But, if they are not being trained and equipped for
each promotion, and if they are not developing Next-Level
Habits to keep them at the new level, then they will not be
able to stay at that new level. If they do not have a functioning Personal Growth Plan, then we will promote good
people to the place called incompetence!

We will all go through times of incompetence, but we don't have to stay there if we have a functioning Personal Growth Plan!

This is an example of what happened in my life. I was a faithful helper, so my team leader promoted me to the position of assistant to a department head. After a while, I did so well that they gave me my own department. Within a couple of years, I was promoted again. This time they gave me three departments. Several years later, they placed me over eight departments. I was a rising star on the leadership team; then, from what seemed like out of nowhere, I was incompetent.

We are growing to where we are going, or we are not going anywhere.

It was so easy for me to handle multiple departments, but somewhere between eight and sixteen departments, I became incompetent. Then the talk starts, "What has happened to Eddie?"

"He was a great leader, but it's obvious that something's definitely wrong with him."

The real problem was that I had been promoted to incompetence. I was not being trained and equipped for each new level. I did not have a functioning Personal Growth Plan. I was not developing Next-Level Habits in my life. The good news was that I made the appropriate changes and rose even higher in leadership. Always set targets; don't set limits.

I have always taken the position that my personal development is my responsibility. Any help I get from my leader is a bonus!

If a person is not trained for each new level, then they will be promoted to incompetence!

So what is a Personal Growth Plan? A Personal Growth Plan would consist of a program of equipping tools: a good church, books, tapes, training CDs, videos, college classes, conferences, workshops, and leadership training classes. Good provisional relationships are also very important because we all need someone that can mentor and model us.

You must learn to anticipate your move in advance and prepare for it. Get a sense for what God is doing in your life and prepare for it.

Can I challenge you today to develop a Personal Growth Plan for your life? You need to take action steps, make calculated preparations, and determine to commit to a process of growth. You need to develop your strategy, refine your strategy, and get committed to that strategy. Your victory is found in your strategy!

CHAPTER

13

CAPACITY INCREASER: NEXT-LEVEL HABITS

To increase my Personal Capacity, I must develop NEXT-LEVEL HABITS!

When most people hear the word "habit," it relays a negative thought or reaction in them! Most people relate the word "habit" to all those failed attempts to lose twenty undesired pounds. The truth is that habits have gotten a bad rap. You see habits are neither good nor bad. Habits are a lot like money. In itself, money has no morality, but a person can produce a byproduct from money that can produce a morality.

> **If a person is not trained for each new level, then they will be promoted to incompetence!**

Money can be used to purchase items like food to feed the hungry, or a drug dealer can use it to buy bullets. Whether or not a habit is good or bad is totally up to each person. I believe God gave us habits as an empowering force, for assisting us in walking in our destiny!

I know what you're thinking. If habits are so great, then why do they give a person so much trouble? Well think about it like this; habits surround a person's life, holding them at their current level.

Diagram #7

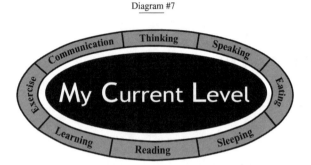

Every time a person tries to rise to the next level, their old habits pull them right back to the previous level. This is exactly what habits were created to do! Habits were designed to bring stability to our lives.

Diagram #8

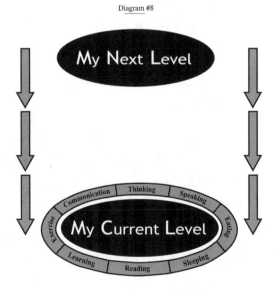

Habits are like gravity.
It takes a lot of energy to break free
from the law of gravity.

It takes all the energy a person can muster together to break free from their old habits. Honestly, most people will ultimately do what their strongest habits tell them to do, good or bad. If you have powerful positive habits, then you will do what those habits tell you to do. If you have powerful negative habits, then you will do what those habits tell you to do.

In Romans 7:15, the Apostle Paul said, "I don't understand what I am doing. I don't do what I want to do, but I do what I don't want to do."

The Apostle Paul also said something very interesting in Philippians 3:13-15 (ESV), "[this] one thing I do!"

> *Brothers, I do not consider that I have made it. But one thing I do: forgetting what lies behind and straining forward to what lies ahead,*
> *I press on toward the goal for the prize of the upward call of God in Christ Jesus.*
> *Let those of us, who are mature think this way,*

At first glance, it looks like Paul has made a mistake. He boldly declares, "[this] one thing I do," but then he goes on to tell us two things. First, he tells us to forget what lies behind. Then, he tells us that he strains forward to what lies ahead. Paul clearly states not one thing but two. I think Paul knew a person could not focus on two different destinations. Next-Level Habits work the same way. I strengthen my new Next-Level Habit and ignore my present habits. I feed my Next-Level Habit and starve my existing habits.

Next-Level Habits are not the habits I need to be successful today, but the habits I will need to be a success next month, a success next year!

The habits you choose empower and advance your life, or the habits you choose stifle and destroy your life! Notice that I said the habits you choose. I choose my habits; I don't let habits choose me. Here is an example of how to form good habits.

First, choose the habits you want in your life. When you change your habits, your habits change you.

Step one:
I pick out my destination.

- The kind of spouse I want to be.
- The kind of parent I want to be.
- The kind of employee I want to be.
- The kind of leader I want to be.
- The quality of communicator I want to be.
- The kind of businessperson I want to be.

Step two:
I now make a list of the habits needed to operate at that next level or position.

- Thinking habit.
- Speaking habit.
- Eating habit.
- Sleeping habit.
- Reading habit.
- Learning habit.
- Communication habit.
- Exercise habit.

It's not always easy to know what a person's Next-Level Habit should look like. So I suggest that you start watching people who are functioning successfully at a level or position that you are desiring. I would also note any bad habits they might have that are limiting them.

I don't worry about my old habits. I let my new Next-Level Habits deal with my old habits!

Step three:
Start feeding your Next-Level Habits and starving your current habits you want to replace. I want to recommend that you take on two or three new habits at a time. Don't try starting ten new habits all at one time.

Diagram #9

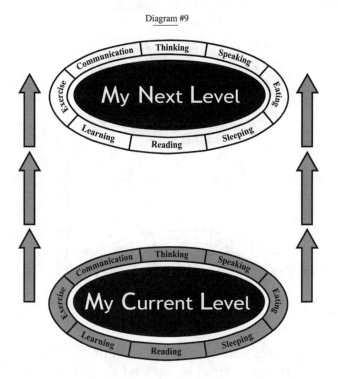

**Focus all your energy and effort on
your desired Next-Level Habits.**

**Do not focus on your existing habits.
Let your Next-Level Habits break your old habits!**

Once you have your desired destination picked out and have made a list of the Next-Level Habits needed to get there, it's time to go to work. I don't wait until I'm at the next level to get started; I start developing and strengthening my new Next-Level Habits right now, and they carry me to my next level. I don't worry about my old habits. I have proven in my life over and over again that I am no match for my old habits. I let my new Next-Level Habits deal with my old habits!

Diagram #10

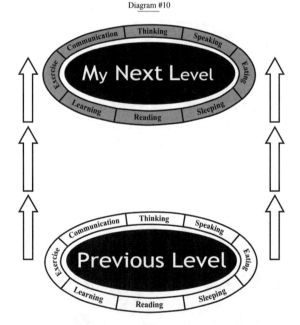

When my son Daniel was about to turn sixteen years old, he decided that he wanted a car. Dad could see right away that this was going to be difficult for Daniel.

You see, Daniel had what we call a bad-spending habit and no savings habit. Daniel loved to play video games. In fact, he had what I would call a fatal attraction for video games. It really didn't matter how much money Daniel had in his wallet because the video game got it all. I knew that if my son was ever going to get the car he desired, I needed to help him develop a Next-Level savings habit. So I took Daniel car shopping.

We went shopping until we found the perfect car. Next, we went to a wheel and tire company and got a price for the perfect wheels and tires. Then, we went to a car stereo store and got a price on the car stereo system of his dreams. We had designed the ultimate car for my son.

I then said to Daniel, "Your mother and I are going to help you buy this car, son! And this is how we are going to do it. Mom and Dad will match every dollar you earn and put in savings for your new car up to three thousand dollars."

I can still see the puzzled look on my son's face as he said, "Dad, I thought you were going to help me get this car?"

I replied, "We will pay up to three thousand dollars on a six thousand dollar car."

Daniel was quiet for several minutes. Then he said, "This could take forever." I told him that I thought that he could save the money in about three to four months if he really applied himself. Daniel was reluctant, but he finally said, "OK!"

Daniel went to work saving his money. He would save fifty dollars and then one hundred fifty dollars only to take it back out of the bank and spend it all. He would then start over and save one hundred fifty dollars and then two hundred fifty dollars only to see something he wanted and spend it all again. He did this over and over again for several months. But never once did I say a negative word to him.

> **Many parents attack their child's bad habits, driving a wedge between the parent and the child.**

This is when most parents really mess things up. They attack their child's bad habits, driving a wedge between the parent and the child. I would keep Daniel focused on his desired destination. I would help him feed and encourage his new Next-Level savings habit and starve his old spending habits. Finally, Daniel saved seven hundred dollars, and we matched it with seven hundred dollars more. Then, he borrowed one thousand dollars and purchased a car for two thousand five hundred dollars. Daniel was so excited as we drove his new car home from the car dealer.

As we drove home that day, I said to Daniel, "Is this the car you really wanted?"

He said, "Dad, you know it is not the car I really wanted because I didn't have enough money."

I told Daniel, "I think we should get the car that you really want, and this is how we can do it. Mom and Dad will match every dollar you put in savings up to three thousand dollars towards your next car. Son, if you will take great care of this car, then I think you will be able to get all your money back when you go to sell it."

In the first two months, Daniel paid back the one thousand dollar loan. Within four months, Daniel had saved one thousand dollars, so Tammy and I matched his one thousand dollars with our one thousand dollars. He did sell his first car for two thousand seven hundred fifty dollars, a two hundred fifty dollar profit. Daniel was so excited to drive home his second car, a Honda De Sol, a two-door convertible!

But as we drove the new car towards home, I said, "Daniel, is this the car you ultimately wanted?"

He said, "Dad, you know it's not the car I really wanted, but it's a great car."

I told Daniel, "I think you should get the car you really wanted, and this is how you can do it. Mom and I will match every dollar you put in savings up to three thousand dollars towards your next car.

Daniel turned to me with a smile on his face and said, "This time, Dad, I will save all three thousand dollars. So you better start saving your three thousand dollars."

Daniel has told several of his friends, "My dad is my coach and financial adviser. You should talk to him before you make big financial decisions."

One day when I was in the United Kingdom, I received a call from Daniel's girlfriend at that time. She said, "Mr. Windsor, I know you have been helping Daniel develop a savings habit, but Mr. Windsor, can you tell Daniel that he doesn't need to save every single dollar he makes! Can you encourage him to spend a little money from time to time on other things?" Daniel made the successful transition from a bad habit to a Next-Level Habit.

Many parents attack their child's bad habits instead of helping their child develop Next-Level Habits.

Once a person has developed their Next-Level Habits, those habits will carry them with less effort to their desired destination! Now listen to me, I didn't say making a new habit would be easy! Making Next-Level Habits will be very difficult! It will take all the discipline and determination you can pull together. But when you finally have your new habits in place, they will take over and carry you to finish the job. You will successfully arrive at your next level.

Why do so many people fail in life when they finally reach their desired destination? They don't have the Next-Level Habits in place to keep them there! If you arrive at the next level for your life but your habits are back at the previous level, guess what? You're on your way back to the previous level.

CHAPTER
14

CAPACITY LIMITERS

**To increase my Personal Capacity,
I must identify my CAPACITY LIMITATIONS!**

There are two kinds of limitations that we will talk about in this chapter. First, there are Capacity Limiters a person can do nothing about. Let's say Bill wanted to be a professional basketball player. But Bill has a limitation. The average height of a professional basketball player is approximately 6'8" tall. Bill is 5'4" tall. This is a limitation Bill can do nothing about. The second type of Capacity Limiter is limitations a person can do something about. Let's say Bill wants a top management job. But Bill has a limitation. Bill has minimal management skills. But this is a limitation he could do something about.

Let's look at four limitations affecting a person's life that they can do something about.

(1) Thinking Limitations

Most people want to live in the present while walking towards their future. They want to live a large and an expansive life. So, what is their limitation? Their memory keeps them tied to their past, stealing their future!

Proverbs 23:7

"For as a man thinks in his heart, so is he."

This verse is clearly telling us that a person is the product of their thinking! They become what they continually think about! You become your thoughts, and your thoughts become you!

So how can the past limit a person's future? Yesterday, Tammy and I were talking about a friend who was raised in the country. Tammy made the old familiar comment, "It is easier to take the boy out of the country than it is to take the country out of the boy."

My parents were raised during the Great Depression. And from time to time, when my dad was doing business with a person that had a very hard time letting go of their money, my dad would call them "depression kids." My dad would tell me, "Their memory of the Depression is stronger than the two hundred thousand dollars cash in their bank account." A mind-set is simply a preconditioned way of thinking.

Because of a mind-set, your preconditioned thinking will not allow you to think a new thought that will give you a better future.

Tammy has worked to help women that have had traumatic experiences in life. Many have suffered sexual abuse, physical abuse, mental abuse, or disease. Tammy has discovered that it is easier to get the women out of the abuse than it is to get the abuse out of the women.

Negative experiences have the potential of leaving their residue on you.

Tammy was the victim of abuse early in her life. It was the kind of abuse that had the potential to leave scars in Tammy for the rest of her life. But Tammy worked hard not to let these experiences take hold of her life. She knew that if they got lodged in her mind, then they would become harder and harder to overcome.

Tammy has been told that she does not even carry the residue of her past experiences in her life. If you smoke, you carry the residue of the cigarette smoke on you. If you have a fire in your home, you can put out the fire, but the residue may stick around for a long time. The negative experiences of your past have the potential to leave their residue on you. It is important that a person understands this residue is left in the form of their thoughts. Your thoughts produce thinking patterns, which in turn produce behavior patterns.

If a person holds onto past experiences in their thinking, it will become a limitation to them.

(2) Skills Limitations

I travel around the world, speaking in hundreds of churches. I cannot tell you how many times people have asked me to believe with them for a new job or a higher paying job. I have asked people over and over again, "Are you qualified for the job or the promotion you are praying for?" I think it's a reasonable question, but far too often, they do not have the skills to match the job they desire.

Ecclesiastes 10:10

"If the ax is dull, And one does not sharpen the edge, Then he must use more strength; But wisdom brings success."

Many years ago, Tammy wanted to get a higher paying job. We prayed for a new job and she put in a job resume. She worked hard trying to get hired on with a company that offered a higher pay scale but with no success. This went on for several years. We had been told several times that she needed more education and more qualifications. Our problem was that we could not afford for her to go back to school. We had two children, a house payment, and two car payments. Our lifestyle was set. Finally, we decided that there was no other way. She was going to need to keep her regular job and go to night school.

So we both worked all day on our regular jobs. We spent the late afternoon with the children, and after dinner, I would get the children ready for bed while Tammy drove forty-five minutes to school. She did this three nights a week. It was a forty-five-minute drive to school and three hours of class time followed by a forty-five-minute drive home. It was a very difficult year for the Windsors. But after one year of additional college, Tammy was now overqualified for the original job she had desired. The good news was that Tammy got a wonderful job at a very high pay rate. She took the time to sharpen the ax! She removed her skill limitation.

(3) Resource Limitations

Most people I talk to have a desire to get out of debt. So what is their limitation? They cannot control their spending. They refuse to live within their means, thus continually overspending.

Remember the story of Elisha and the widow's oil in chapter five? What if Elisha would have said to the little widow, "What are we going to be able to do with a little bit of oil? Get real lady!" But he didn't say that. I love the fact that Elisha did not put the little widow down for her response, "a little bit of oil." He simply asked what resources she had available to her. He needed to know her resource limitation.

When Tammy and I were newly married, we wanted to invest and make extra money. But we had a clear limitation. We had no extra money to invest! This was a clear and undeniable limitation. But one day, I realized that we did have a resource. It was the equity in our home. We had lived in this home for almost ten years. Ten years I had worked on this fixer-upper home. I was so surprised to find out that we had over sixty thousand dollars in equity in our home. In the next couple of months, we sold that home and removed our resource limitation.

Increasing your capacity starts by identifying what resources you have available to you and applying stewardship to those resources.

Have you ever heard the saying, "How do you eat an elephant? One bite at a time!" Increasing your resources starts with identifying the resources you currently have available to you. It turned out that the equity in my home and my Personal Capacity both increased simultaneously, removing my resource limitation.

(4) Relationship Limitations

I have heard it said that a person is only as good as the people that surround them.

Who I am, determines who I am in a relationship with, and who I am in a relationship with, determines who I am!

Let me give you an example. Let's say that a young man is having a problem with pornography and lustful thoughts. So he goes to a close friend and tells him his problem in confidence. Let's say this friend tells him, "Hey man, don't beat yourself up. All guys have problems with pornography." He goes on to say, "As long as you don't get hooked on it, you'll be OK." That friend just limited his potential—he helped him lower his Threshold of Hard. But let's say he goes to a different friend instead and he says, "Hey man, pornography will take you down a road that you don't want to go down. You'll ultimately pay a price you won't want to pay." Many men have had their marriages and families destroyed by pornography. This young man needed a friend that would help him overcome. A friend that will say, "When you are feeling tempted, call me, and I will encourage you. You can break this habit, I believe in you!"

It's easy to see that your friends have the potential to either lift or limit your life. Let me give you a little assignment. Make a list of your relationships and put them in two categories: relationships that lift and challenge you to be more than you presently are, and relationships that limit you.

15

LIFE SYNC

In this book, I have given you important keys enabling you to increase your Personal Capacity. You need to understand that every person has a Personal Capacity, but more importantly, I want you to know that every person has the ability to increase that capacity.

Several years ago, I started the journey of expanding my Personal Capacity. I worked very hard on the process of increasing my Personal Capacity, but if I was to be perfectly honest, when I finally achieved the Personal Capacity I had always dreamed of, something was still missing. At this point, I thought I needed to just work harder! Then I started working longer! I did everything I could to lift my life to the next level, but I was still unsuccessful.

At this point, people start to question themselves. They begin to question their personal ability. They ask questions like, "What's wrong with me?" Next, a person will become frustrated and disillusioned. They soon will lose hope, and their creativity will begin to fade. All this can happen in a person's life even after they have increased their Personal Capacity.

I have identified and have integrated six key areas in my life that gave me the breakthrough I was looking for!

I want you to know that I believe in the increasing of a person's capacity. But if you only increase your capacity, that is not enough! If you want to experience true success in life, then there are multiple areas of your life that must be developed simultaneously. I call this process Life Sync.

I honestly believe that if you will apply Life Sync to your life, then you will have that breakthrough you have always wanted!

<u>My definition of Life Sync</u>:
Integrating multiple key areas in your life producing synergy for a greater Personal Capacity.
৵৶
Synchronized Energy functioning correctly in an individual's life has the potential to create a significant Personal Capacity.

The more areas of your life you can bring into the arena of Life Sync, the greater exponential breakthrough you will experience in your life, thus producing personal synergy.

I also apply Life Sync when I pray! Each time I pray, I bring these three areas into "Sync:" the prayer of faith, the power of agreement, and the authority of the Word. Many people pray but not in faith. A husband and wife might pray together, but secretly they may not be in agreement. And far too often people are praying prayers that are not in agreement with the authority of God's Word. People ask me all the time, "How does God speak to you?" It's simple! God is a Spirit, so when He speaks, it is in the Spirit. That is why we hear it in our spirit, and we call it "the inward witness" or "the still, small voice."

Here are the six areas in my life where I apply the Life Sync principles that help produce personal synergy.

(1) Alignment of my Personal Values

What are values? They are a person's most important fundamental core beliefs. Values provide a person with the guidance system needed to organize their life. Values are based on the principle, the purpose, the conviction, the ideal, and the belief that you use to guide your life.

I guess you're wondering why I have chosen values first. You must understand and identify your values before you can formulate meaningful goals that help you develop your Personal Growth Plan.

Defining your values gives you the passion and focus to pursue realistic, purposeful, and meaningful goals!

If a person wants to see true success they must position themselves in a place aligned with their personal values. Let me give you a couple of my personal values: my marriage, my family, and my church are at the center of my world. All my life, quality marriages, godly marriages, have been modeled for me. My grandparents were married for over sixty-five years, my parents have been married for almost sixty years, and Tammy and I have been married for twenty-two years. These marriages were all to one spouse, not accumulated over multiple marriages!

One evening, I was on a flight from London to Detroit. The man sitting in the seat next to me was very talkative, and he asked 101 questions. He had asked if I was married and for how long. I love it when people ask me how long I've been married. I proudly said, "Twenty-two years!"

He boldly announced that he had been married thirty-eight years! I said, "Really, your wife looks too young to have been married for thirty-eight years!"

He said, "No, we have been married only six years; the thirty-eight years is an accumulation over six marriages!" Needless to say, I was speechless.

If a person wants to see true success, then they must position themselves in a place aligned with their personal values.

I understand that the quality of my marriage and family is enhanced by the quality of my relationship with God and my church. I cannot stress to you enough how important it is to identify and understand your personal values. Knowing and understanding your personal values is the first step towards applying Life Sync!

(2) Expansion of my Personal Capacity

Every person on the planet has a Personal Capacity, and I am constantly aware of my current capacity. However, more importantly I am aware of my need to increase that capacity. I realize that the dream in my heart and the things I desire to accomplish in my family, in my ministry, and in my business is tied to the level of my Personal Capacity. I will talk more about Personal Capacity in the next few chapters.

(3) Alignment of my Provisional Relationships

This is my definition of Provisional Relationships. It is those relationships that the provision of God flows through into our lives, enabling us to live healthy, successful, and fulfilled for the purpose of fulfilling our destiny in God.

It is important to understand that your pastor is the number one provision of a God relationship in your life. There are other relationships that can become provision of God relationships over time or for different seasons of your life.

You must also understand that it is your responsibility to align yourself with Provisional Relationships, not the other way around.

Jesus was a Provisional Relationship in the lives of the disciples. Elijah was that relationship to Elisha.

2 Kings 2:2

"Elisha said to Elijah, 'As the LORD lives, and as your soul lives, I will not leave you!'"

It was Elisha's responsibility to stay connected to Elijah. It was the disciple's responsibility to stay connected to Jesus. It is your responsibility to stay connected to your Provisional Relationship.

(4) Discipline of my Next-Level Habits

Next-Level Habits are not the habits I need to be successful today, but they are the habits I will need to be successful next month, next year, or in ten years! The truth is that you will ultimately do what your strongest habits tell you to do!

Apostle Paul said, "Those things I don't want to do I do but those things I do want to do I don't do!"

This is how I create successful habits in my life. I feed my Next-Level Habits and starve my existing habits. I empower my Next-Level Habits, and my new habits override my old habits. Why do so many people fail in life when they finally reach their desired destination? They don't have the habits in place to keep them there! In my life, Next-Level Habits have played a vital part in my success.

(5) Refinement and implementation of my Personal Growth Plan

We are growing to where we are going, or we are not going anywhere. Jesus paid the price for your salvation, but you will pay the price to go to the next level in your life.

**A Personal Growth Plan is a crucial part of
your Personal Capacity Guidance System.**

A Personal Growth Plan will help you make calculated and purposeful plans, and it will help you stay
determined and committed to your growth process. You
need to develop your strategy, refine it, and get committed to it. Your victory is found in your strategy.

(6) Lifting my Hard Threshold

My definition of the Law of Hard: Whatever you
find hard in life has the potential to temporarily and/or
permanently define your life, your business, and your
ministry.

I am sure you have heard of a "threshold of pain."
A year ago, my son, Daniel, had emergency surgery.
After the surgery, the doctor asked Daniel if he had been
in very much pain. Daniel told him that he had a little
discomfort before the operation, but it wasn't too bad.
The doctor told Daniel that his condition is one of those
that produce a high level of pain. The doctor said, "You
have a high threshold of pain!"

Now my wife, on the other hand, has a lower
threshold of pain. If she even thinks there might be some
pain, she's concerned.

We all have a threshold of pain, and in a very similar way, we all have a Threshold of Hard.

> ### My definition of the Threshold of Hard:
>
> It is that point when your life, business, and ministry challenges stop you from lifting your life to the next level because of an inability to solve the challenges at that next level.

Every person has a Hard Threshold, and I am always aware that I must be continually lifting that threshold.

CHAPTER

16

LIFE SYNC APPLICATION

So how do we apply Life Sync to multiple areas of our life?

Step one: Define your Focus

What do you really want to achieve in your life? What is your passion? What is the deep desire of your heart? Where do you get a sense of God's leading? What are you good at that produces results in your life?

Step two: Refine your Focus

You cannot walk in two directions at the same time. The Apostle Paul said, "This one thing I do!" Identify a general direction you would need to go in to obtain your desires or passion. Limit your time, talent, and money towards advancing those specific areas.

Step three: Streamline your Focus

Eliminate activities in your life that will distract and hinder your progress towards your desired destination. Focus on developing your habits, skills, and abilities that you will need to reach that next level. And also, target and focus the spending of your money that will get you to where you desire to go.

Step four: Engage your Focus

Once you know your desired direction you want to go, and you have streamlined your life in order to be able to have the resources and the knowledge to get you there, take calculated and precise action steps toward your focused destination.

Let's take a young man I am currently mentoring through the Life Sync process. His name is Samuel, and he attends Wisdom for Life Leadership School at my home church, Covenant Celebration Church, where Kevin and Sheila Gerald are the Senior Pastors. Samuel has learned that the first step in the Life Sync process is to define his life's focus—where does he want to go, what does he want to do in life, and what talents does he have. He has identified that his passion in life is to be in full-time ministry.

> **Life Sync creates momen-tum towards your desired destination.**

The next step is to refine his focus. Samuel's identification of his passion for full-time ministry is still too broad. What area of ministry does he have a passion for?

Does he want to be an office manager, an accountant, a worship leader, or a children's pastor? He must refine his focus. Samuel has defined that he wants to be a youth pastor. This will now help Samuel to know where to spend his time and energy.

Now Samuel must streamline his focus! What is he currently doing to get him moving towards his passion? Is he being distracted by good causes, like working in the music department, the nursery, or administration? Samuel must identify those areas that are not taking him where he needs to go. Even though they are good things to spend time on and though he may be needed there, he must eliminate them in order to achieve his ultimate passion. Samuel must have a sense by now of where God would have him go and begin to prepare for that destination.

Then, last but not least, what will be the action steps that Samuel will need to take to be a full-time youth pastor?

Below is the Personal Capacity Assessment Profile that I have done on Samuel over the last several months. Based on what he has communicated to me and what I have observed, these are the ratings that I have compiled. Samuel has stated that his desired destination in life thus far is to be in full-time ministry as a youth pastor. Now based on that destination, I observe each area.

Example: When I look at Samuel's habits, I have determined that if he does not change his current habits, then he will have approximately a 40 percent chance of fulfilling his desired destination. Then when I look at his Personal Growth Plan, it looks awesome on paper, and I give the plan approximately an 80 percent chance of getting him to his desired destination. So on and so on through each area.

Now let's apply the Life Sync principles to see how they can produce personal synergy in Samuel's life.

For this illustration:

- Addition represents working on different areas of life independently.
- Multiplication represents working on multiple areas of life simultaneously.

Example: Applying Life Sync in two areas of Samuel's life at one time.

Personal Values
1 2 3 4 5 6 7 8 **(9)** 10

Personal Capacity
1 2 3 4 5 6 7 **(8)** 9 10

$9 + 8 = 17$

Personal Values plus our Personal Capacity Rating, without applying Life Sync, equals seventeen.

$9 \times 8 = 72$

Personal Values plus our Personal Capacity Rating, while applying Life Sync equals a total of seventy-two. Life Sync produced a four times greater Personal Capacity rating.

Example: Applying Life Sync in three areas of Samuel's life at one time.

Personal Values
1 2 3 4 5 6 7 8 (9) 10

Personal Capacity
1 2 3 4 5 6 7 (8) 9 10

Provisional Relationships
1 2 3 4 5 6 (7) 8 9 10

9 + 8 + 7 = 24 (rating without Life Sync)
9 x 8 x 7 = 504 (rating with Life Sync)

Life Sync produced a twenty-one times greater Personal Capacity rating.

Example: Applying Life Sync in four areas of Samuel's life at one time.

Personal Values
1 2 3 4 5 6 7 8 (9) 10

Personal Capacity
1 2 3 4 5 6 7 (8) 9 10

Provisional Relationships
1 2 3 4 5 6 (7) 8 9 10

Next-Level Habits
1 2 3 (4) 5 6 7 8 9 10

9 + 8 + 7 + 4 = 28 (rating without Life Sync)
9 x 8 x 7 x 4 = 2016 (rating with Life Sync)

Life Sync produced a seventy-two times greater Personal Capacity rating.

Example: Applying Life Sync in five areas of Samuel's life at one time.

Personal Values
1 2 3 4 5 6 7 8 (9) 10

Personal Capacity
1 2 3 4 5 6 7 (8) 9 10

Provisional Relationships
1 2 3 4 5 6 (7) 8 9 10

Next-Level Habits
1 2 3 (4) 5 6 7 8 9 10

Personal Growth Plan
1 2 3 4 5 6 7 (8) 9 10

9 + 8 + 7 + 4 + 8 = 36 (rating without Life Sync)
9 x 8 x 7 x 4 x 8 = 16,128 (rating with Life Sync)

Life Sync produced a four hundred forty-eight times greater Personal Capacity rating.

Example: Applying Life Sync in six areas of Samuel's life at one time.

Personal Values
1 2 3 4 5 6 7 8 (9) 10

Personal Capacity
1 2 3 4 5 6 7 (8) 9 10

Provisional Relationships
1 2 3 4 5 6 (7) 8 9 10

Next-Level Habits
1 2 3 (4) 5 6 7 8 9 10

Personal Growth Plan
1 2 3 4 5 6 7 (8) 9 10

Hard Threshold
1 2 3 4 (5) 6 7 8 9 10

$9 + 8 + 7 + 4 + 8 + 5 = 41$ (rating without Life Sync)
$9 \times 8 \times 7 \times 4 \times 8 \times 5 = 80{,}640$ (rating with Life Sync)

Life Sync produced an almost two thousand times greater Personal Capacity rating.

Now let's walk through how Samuel has applied the Life Sync principles to his everyday life.

(1) The alignment of his Personal Values!

Remember Samuel's values are the guidance system needed to organize his life. He must understand and identify his values before he can formulate meaningful goals and his Personal Growth Plan.

- Samuel's core value is integrity, which is lived out in his mission statement: "To know God, build and inspire integrity in others through modeling a lifestyle of passion for God."

This is the guidance system through which he filters his ministry and life decisions.

(2) Expansion of his Personal Capacity!

- Samuel is committed to his church and to the application of the training he receives.
- Samuel is attending Wisdom for Life Leadership School.
- Samuel volunteers as an intern for the junior high youth ministry.
- Samuel has established his life and ministry mentors.

If Samuel wanted to be a singer, then he would get voice lessons. If he wanted to be an accountant, then he would take accounting classes. It is important to keep your time and energy focused like a laser on your targeted destination. The Bible says that Jesus had His eye set as flint on His desired destination.

(3) Alignment of his Provisional Relationships

- Samuel values and is committed to his local church and to the application of the wisdom and training from his pastor. He knows that his local church is God's plan for refinement and alignment of life and ministry.
- Samuel is committed to follow the counsel of Frank Washburn, Director of Wisdom for Life Leadership School. Based on Samuel's desire for full-time youth ministry, Frank has helped Samuel map out the journey for increasing his Personal Capacity.
- Samuel will receive hands-on application in ministry training from John Morgan in the area of youth ministry. John is known as one of the best youth pastors in ministry today. Everyone knows

John is serious about youth ministry, and he will stretch Samuel in ways that he has never been stretched before. Under the guidance of Pastor John, Samuel will see his personal gifts and talents increase and go to the next level needed to be successful in youth ministry.

- Samuel has asked me to be his Life and Ministry Mentor. I will start by working on Samuel's personal lifestyle. I will be helping him to develop personal Next-Level Habits that will be the foundation for his success in life and ministry. I will be working with him to keep him focused on his ministry goals, while lifting his Hard Threshold.

(4) Discipline of his Next-Level Habits!

Samuel is establishing Next-Level Habits based on his focused destination. How does this work?

- First, Samuel will set goals based on his defined focus.
- Next, he will set up a Personal Growth Plan to increase his Personal Capacity, enabling him to reach his goals. He will need to write out realistic and purposeful goals to help guide him on his journey. For those days when his destination is unattainable, he can use his goals as a way to help him stay going in the right direction. Goals help us to stay on course.
- Samuel now establishes Next-Level Habits around his Personal Growth Plan. What are the habits he will need, to get to where he wants to go?

(5) Refinement and implementation of his Personal Growth Plan!

Samuel's Personal Growth Plan is a crucial part of Life Sync. His Personal Growth Plan is under constant refinement. He always has a one-year plan in motion, but he knows that if his Personal Growth Plan is not giving him his desired results, then he makes adjustments. It is important to remember that your Personal Growth Plan works for you; you don't work for it.

- Samuel identifies where he is spending his time, energy, and money. He eliminates the areas that are not taking him towards being in full-time ministry.
- Samuel begins to work on his physical appearance. He is doing this through changing his fashion and hairstyle. He is now wearing braces to fix his teeth. He is learning that to connect with youth you must be relevant and able to identify with their culture.
- Samuel is attending conferences, speaking for youth groups in other local churches. He is taking communication and preaching courses in leadership school. He is working academically to train himself for where he is going.

(6) Lifting of his Hard Threshold

For this point I will use an illustration to show how important it is for Samuel to lift his Hard Threshold.

Using our Personal Capacity Rating System, this is Samuel's evaluation.

Personal Values
1 2 3 4 5 6 7 8 (9) 10

Personal Capacity
1 2 3 4 5 6 7 (8) 9 10

Provisional Relationships
1 2 3 4 5 6 (7) 8 9 10

Next-Level Habits
2 3 4 5 (6) 7 8 9 10

Personal Growth Plan
1 2 3 4 5 6 7 8 (9) 10

Hard Threshold
1 2 3 4 (5) 6 7 8 9 10

I will use a white Styrofoam cup full of water to illustrate this thought. First, I will put a mark on the outside of the cup around the 80 percent full level to represent Samuel's current personal ability (Personal Capacity). Secondly, I will put marks at 90 percent, 70 percent, 60 percent and 90 percent representing his Personal Values, Provisional Relationships, his Next-Level Habits and his Personal Growth Plan. Finally, I will put a mark at the 50 percent level to represent his Hard Threshold.

It has been my experience that most people focus 99 percent of their efforts on their personal abilities and little if any effort on other vital areas of personal development. Building your personal ability without building Provisional Relationships, Next-Level Habits, a Personal Growth Plan, and an adequate Hard Threshold is like a pilot asking the passengers, "Where would you like to go today?" I have never had a pilot ask me where I want to go! His voice comes over the intercom and gives us the flight plan. "We will leave the gate at 10:45 A.M. We will cruise at an altitude of thirty-eight thousand feet. Our flying time today is twelve hours and thirteen minutes. We will arrive ten minutes ahead of schedule at gate N16." We will successfully reach our desired destination because our pilot has a prepared and approved flight plan. And you will only reach your desired destination with a growth plan for your life.

Back to our white Styrofoam cup illustration. Remember that Samuel's current ability is at 80 percent, but his Hard Threshold is much lower at 50 percent. Samuel is shocked to find out that the 30 percent of his personal ability above his Hard Threshold could potentially be lost.

If I now take a knife and place a cut in our Styrofoam cup at the 50 percent Hard Threshold mark, what happens? Water begins to run out onto the floor. All of Samuel's hard work developing his abilities, capacity, and his growth plan can potentially be lost unless he can raise his Hard Threshold to match his other ratings.

Let's now take a pitcher of water representing more effort, more education, and more training and pour more water into the top of our cup. You guessed it—the water just runs out at Samuel's Hard Threshold level.

At this point, Samuel begins to get frustrated! He begins to think, "I need more training, I need more education, I need to work harder, and I need to work longer." He's starting to say things like, "Maybe I'm not cut out for this." Honestly, all he needs to do is lift his Hard

Threshold to match the rest of his capacity ratings. It doesn't matter how much education a person has because if it's too hard for them to get out of bed in the mornings and get to work on time, they won't keep their job anyway! They could have several degrees and a Ph.D. certificate hanging on their wall, but if they cannot lift their Hard Threshold, then all of their degrees are useless.

At this point, Samuel has embarked on a journey called Life Sync. He has a desire to increase his Personal Capacity. So he continually lifts his personal ability, while in sync with his values, that are in sync with his Provisional Relationships, that are in sync with his Next-Level Habits, that are in sync with his Personal Growth Plan, that are in sync with his Hard Threshold. Samuel has Life Sync working in his life producing the environment and potential for many breakthroughs in his life and ministry journey.

CHAPTER 17

TEAM SYNC

L ife Sync is the way to accomplish true success for individuals. However, I believe Team Sync is the key for accomplishing true success for teams.

> **My definition of Team Sync:**
> **Integrating the Personal Capacity, skill and competence of all team members producing synergy for a greater team capacity.**
>
> ❧⟶❦
>
> **Synchronized Energy functioning correctly among a group of individuals has the potential to create a significant team capacity.**

The Bible tells us that one can put one thousand to flight, but two can put ten thousand to flight. With the help of Team Sync, a group of ordinary people can accomplish extraordinary things!

I guess the question that comes to everyone's mind is, "If Team Sync works that well, then why do so many teams fail?" My question would be, "Does putting a group of individuals together and calling them a team produce Team Sync?"

Let's look at the potential difference between "Working Together" and "Team Sync."

For our illustration, I will use *addition* to represent a group of five people working together as individuals and *multiplication* to represent a group of five people working together producing Team Sync.

- Addition = Working together as individuals
- Multiplication = Team Sync

$1 + 1 + 1 + 1 + 1 = 5$ POTENTIAL TEAM CAPACITY
$1 \times 1 \times 1 \times 1 \times 1 = 1$ POTENTIAL TEAM CAPACITY

So what did we learn from this illustration? Five people working as individuals produced a five times greater result. What would be another way to explain this result? That it takes five times more effort to produce Team Sync.

- This is the place in our journey where Team Sync has the potential of breaking down. It is more work creating Team Sync than just doing the work as individuals.
- At this point, most people say, "It is easier to do the work myself."
- Many would say, "By the time I teach others, I could have been done with the work and be home with my family."

- A friend said to me, "To tell you the truth, I don't feel anyone on this team can do the job as good as I can!" And he was probably accurate in his assessment.

Well, we have proved one thing. Team Sync will take work, and people that don't understand Team Sync will resist it!

However, before we give up on Team Sync altogether, let's give it one more chance.

Using a scale of 1-10

1 to 3 = Our team really does not understand true Team Sync.
4 to 5 = Our team understands basic Team Sync and its application.
6 to 8 = Our team has a firm grasp of the dynamics of Team Sync and its application.
9 to 10 = Our team has mastered true Team Sync!

Let's return to our illustration.

$$2 + 2 + 2 + 2 + 2 = 10 \text{ POTENTIAL TEAM CAPACITY}$$
$$2 \times 2 \times 2 \times 2 \times 2 = 32 \text{ POTENTIAL TEAM CAPACITY}$$

- Team Sync produced a three times greater Team Capacity.

At this point, our five-member team does not understand Team Sync. They are most likely being forced to work the principles of Team Sync by a team leader, a department head or employer. Our leader sees the benefit of Team Sync and presses the team on!

4 + 4 + 4 + 4 + 4 = 20 POTENTIAL TEAM CAPACITY
4 x 4 x 4 x 4 x 4 = 1,024 POTENTIAL TEAM CAPACITY

- Team Sync produced a fifty-one times greater Team Capacity.

Way to go team! We now have a team that is beginning to understand basic Team Sync and its application. Don't stop now!

6 + 6 + 6 + 6 + 6 = 30 POTENTIAL TEAM CAPACITY
6 x 6 x 6 x 6 x 6 = 7,776 POTENTIAL TEAM CAPACITY

- Team Sync produced a two hundred fifty-nine times greater capacity.

Our team has a firm grasp of the dynamics of Team Sync and its application. Now the team does not need to be pulled along by their leader or pushed by their employer. They are eager to take this new understanding of Team Sync to the next level!

10 + 10 + 10 + 10 + 10 = 50 POTENTIAL TEAM CAPACITY
10 x 10 x 10 x 10 x 10 = 100,000 POTENTIAL TEAM CAPACITY

- Team Sync produced a two thousand times greater team capacity.

Our team of five people working as individuals produced a potential team capacity totaling fifty. They worked harder and harder, and they worked longer and longer! They had accomplishments, but they still worked as individuals! Our team of five people working together using Team Sync produced a one hundred thousand potential team capacity and a two thousand times larger outcome for their efforts.

If we will follow through with the process of Team Sync long enough, then we will begin to see the real benefits of working as a team! The key is going all the way through the Team Sync process.

TEAM SYNC APPLICATION

N ow that we all can see that Team Sync will produce the results needed to accomplish our organizational goals, how do we produce true Team Sync? Let me demonstrate Team Sync with a sports illustration.

I pass you the ball in such a way to maximize your strengths, while you position yourself in such a way to receive the ball to maximize my strengths.

Example: Daniel and Jeremy are on the same football team. Daniel's job on the team is to pass Jeremy the ball. Jeremy's job is to score touchdowns! So Daniel throws the ball to Jeremy, but he puts so little thought into how he passes to Jeremy that the ball is dropped, and no score is made. Jeremy thinks to himself, "What a bad pass! He threw it at my head!" Daniel's thinking, "Come on Jeremy, catch the ball!" This is an example of two people working as individuals on a team. But they both failed to achieve the team objective, which is to get the ball into the end zone and make the score.

So how can our two football players get some Team Sync working? Let's go back to our sports definition of Team Sync. Daniel must pass the ball in such a way as to maximize Jeremy's strengths. So Daniel must know how Jeremy likes to receive the ball. Jeremy tells Daniel, "I like to catch the ball right in the middle of my midsection with both hands." So once again, Daniel throws the ball to Jeremy, but this time, Daniel throws the ball right into Jeremy's midsection so he can catch the ball with both hands! Jeremy makes the catch and is soon tackled. The crowd begins to clap! They had a job to do, and although it wasn't pretty, some progress was made. The boys are excited! But wait a minute, we have one problem: our team's objectives are still not fulfilled. No touchdown was made!

This is an example of Team Sync in its lowest form. Daniel has passed the ball to maximize Jeremy's strengths. So although we have Team Sync working, it is in its lowest form. Let's go back to our definition again. "Daniel must pass the ball in such a way to maximize Jeremy's strengths while Jeremy positions himself in such a way to receive the ball to maximize Daniel's strengths."

So it is not enough for Daniel to know how Jeremy likes to receive the ball. Jeremy must know how Daniel likes to pass the ball and position himself in that place. Daniel likes his receivers to be running left to right in a crossing pattern, angling towards the goal line about thirty yards across the line of scrimmage.

Once again, Daniel passes the ball to Jeremy. Daniel knows that Jeremy is at his best when he can receive a ball thrown into his midsection. Jeremy knows Daniel wants him angling left to right in a crossing pattern thirty yards across the line of scrimmage. Daniel throws the perfect pass, Jeremy makes the perfect catch, he gets the touchdown, and the crowd goes wild!

At one time, this was my definition of Team Sync: Team Sync is nothing more than our attempt to explain what happens when a team is functioning correctly.

Now I understand that although Team Sync is important, it alone does not guarantee success!

I have observed many teams that have a good understanding of Team Sync, but they still do not achieve their desired goals. I know that at this point, it sounds as if I am contradicting myself. Let me explain it like this. Team Sync is one side of a coin. Every coin has two sides. If it has two heads, it is a counterfeit and worthless. So what is the second side of our coin? It is Team Capacity! For our team to be truly effective, we must have a firm grasp of the dynamics of Team Sync and its application as well as Competent Team Capacity.

A person's capacity is based on the skills and competence level needed in their current position and/or considered position.

A person's Personal Capacity is rated on a scale of 1-10.

1 to 3 = INCOMPETENT CAPACITY
4 to 6 = COMPETENT CAPACITY
7 to 10 = NEXT-LEVEL CAPACITY

When we place individuals on a team, they produce a Team Capacity.

CAPACITY ASSESSMENT SYSTEM
PERSONAL & TEAM CAPACITY
A five-person team

	Team Leader	Team Member	Team Member	Team Member	Team Member
INCOMPETENT CAPACITY	1	1	1	1	1
	2	2	2	2	(2)
	3	(3)	(3)	3	3
COMPETENT CAPACITY	4	4	4	4	4
	(5)	5	5	5	5
	6	6	6	6	6
NEXT-LEVEL CAPACITY	7	7	7	(7)	7
	8	8	8	8	8
	9	9	9	9	9
	10	10	10	10	10

Team Capacity

WITHOUT TEAM SYNC PRINCIPLES	$5 + 3 + 3 + 7 + 2 = 20$ TCR*
APPLYING TEAM SYNC PRINCIPLES	$5 \times 3 \times 3 \times 7 \times 2 = 630$ TCR*

*Team Capacity Rating

The first thing I want you to notice in this illustration is that our team leader has a "5" for his Personal Capacity. Although our leader is competent in his leadership position at this time, it is important to understand that he must grow at a rate equal to that of the organization's; otherwise, he will move towards incompetence.

Our next two team members are rated as a "3" in their Personal Capacities. There are several possible reasons for their incompetence. One reason might be that they have not been trained for the position that they are being asked to fulfill. They might have the potential for a greater capacity, but they don't understand the importance of their position, and how their Personal Capacity affects our team's success. It could be that they are not on the right team. It might be that they are on the right team but in the wrong position on our team. It's possible their skill and gifting do not match the position that they are being asked to fill on the team.

Our fourth team member is rated as a "7" in their Personal Capacity. This places them right on the edge of Next-Level Capacity. In a growing organization, it is best if our team leaders have a Next-Level Capacity.

Our final team member has been rated as a "2." It has been my experience that a "2" is almost always placed incorrectly. For example, let's say that on Sunday our team member works as a door greeter welcoming guests to our church. But during the week, his regular job is a drill sergeant in the Marines rated as a "10." If our team member rated as a "2" could work in the church as church security, his personal capacity rating would be much higher. With this change, his capacity rating could move from Incompetent Capacity to Competent Capacity.

What if each team member could lift his or her Personal Capacity just one level higher?

Team Capacity
6 + 4 + 4 + 8 + 3 = 25 TCR - TS
6 x 4 x 4 x 8 x 3 = 2,304 TCR + TS

By lifting their Personal Capacity one level, it produces a 3.5 times greater Team Capacity than the Team Capacity of six hundred thirty.

This is what would happen if each team member could lift his or her Personal Capacity just one more level.

7 + 5 + 5 + 9 + 4 = 30 TCR - TS
7 x 5 x 5 x 9 x 4 = 6,300 TCR + TS

By each team member lifting their Personal Capacity one more level, it produced a ten times greater Team Capacity.

When we increase our Personal Capacity, it not only benefits our personal lives, it also increases our Team Capacity! I don't believe most people realize the personal benefits and team benefits that come from lifting their Personal Capacity just one more level. If each team member does not increase his or her Personal Capacity, then the team's capacity will not increase.

Extraordinary teams are the result of high-capacity team members producing a competent Team Capacity functioning in the highest levels of Team Sync.

Let me illustrate.

- Michael Jordan on a High-Capacity team!

- Michael Jordan on an Average-Capacity team!

CAPACITY ASSESSMENT SYSTEM
PERSONAL & TEAM CAPACITY

Michael Jordan & the World Champion Chicago Bulls

	Michael Jordan	Team Member	Team Member	Team Member	Team Member
INCOMPETENT CAPACITY	1 2 3	1 2 3	1 2 3	1 2 3	1 2 3
COMPETENT CAPACITY	4 5 6	4 5 6	4 5 6	4 5 6	4 5 6
NEXT-LEVEL CAPACITY	7 8 9 (10)	7 8 (9) 10	7 8 (9) 10	7 (8) 9 10	7 (8) 9 10

HIGH-CAPACITY TEAM

$10 \times 9 \times 9 \times 8 \times 8 = 51{,}840$ TCR*
*Team Capacity Rating

I don't need to tell you who the player is that I rated as a ten! It was exciting to watch the Chicago Bulls win six World Championships in seven years. If you know anything about basketball, then you know that it was an extraordinary accomplishment. They were high-capacity individuals that produced a competent Team Capacity while functioning in the highest levels of Team Sync.

Now let's look at Michael Jordan on a second team.

CAPACITY ASSESSMENT SYSTEM
PERSONAL & TEAM CAPACITY

Michael Jordan & the Wizards

	Michael Jordan	Team Member	Team Member	Team Member	Team Member
INCOMPETENT CAPACITY	1 2 3	1 2 3	1 2 3	1 2 3	1 2 3
COMPETENT CAPACITY	4 5 6	4 5 6	4 5 6	4 5 **(6)**	4 **(5)** 6
NEXT-LEVEL CAPACITY	7 8 9 **(10)**	7 **(8)** 9 10	**(7)** 8 9 10	7 8 9 10	7 8 9 10

HIGH-CAPACITY Team
The Bulls
10 x 9 x 9 x 8 x 8 = 51,840 (TCR*)

AVERAGE-CAPACITY Team
The Wizards
10 x 8 x 7 x 6 x 5 = 16,800 (TCR*)
*Team Capacity Rating

I want you to notice something. Every player on the Wizards starting lineup was competent. They had no incompetent players. Their Team Capacity just wasn't high enough. Remember our Team Capacity is a result of the combination of our Personal Capacities. And an individual's capacity is based on the skills and competence levels needed in their current position and/or considered position.

TEAM SYNC & OUR TEAM LEADER

Let me show you the effect Team Sync has on our team. Again, I will use addition to show what happens when our team does not apply Team Sync and multiplication when it does. This is a team of five individuals who have come together applying Team Sync. I have rated each team member at a level five, meaning they all have an Average Competent Capacity.

$$5 \text{ X } 5 \text{ X } 5 \text{ X } 5 \text{ X } 5 = 3,125$$

By applying Team Sync, this team has created a very high Team Capacity rating. However, what if their employer wanted them to have an even higher Team Capacity rating? What if the employer wanted a greater volume of productivity for their efforts? What would happen if the employer replaced one of the team members with a Next-Level Capacity person, someone rated a ten in their Personal Capacity? Would this guarantee a greater Team Capacity? Let's find out!

$$5 \text{ X } 5 \text{ X } 5 \text{ X } 5 + 10 = 635$$

What happened to our team's potential? What has gone wrong? A team member was added with twice the

Personal Capacity, but our team's productivity has been cut by five times. The answer is obvious. Our Next-Level Capacity team member did not sync with the rest of the team.

So now the employer thinks he has a better idea. Let's make our Next-Level Capacity team member the team leader! That will get us our desired results.

$$10 \ + \ 5 \ \times \ 5 \ \times \ 5 \ \times \ 5 = 1{,}875$$

Our Team Capacity rating is better, but it is still almost half of our original team's capacity. I learned a long time ago that if you cannot get along with the team, you cannot be on the team. As John Maxwell often says, "A TEAM is - Together Everyone Achieves More!" The key word is together! For our team to have maximum results and achieve our desired productivity, we must have Team Sync between every member. Now, let's look at the results and see if our Next-Level Capacity team member can Team Sync with the team.

$$10 \ \times \ 5 \ \times \ 5 \ \times \ 5 \ \times \ 5 \ = 6{,}250$$

We have now doubled the original team's potential productivity through Team Sync. But to achieve these results, is it a requirement for the Next-Level Capacity team member to be the leader? Let's see!

$$5 \ \times \ 5 \ \times \ 5 \ \times \ 5 \ \times \ 10 = 6{,}250$$
$$5 \ \times \ 5 \ \times \ 10 \ \times \ 5 \ \times \ 5 = 6{,}250$$

It does not seem to matter where we put the Next-Level Capacity team member. How is this possible? What are the dynamics at work here? It is simply Team Sync! When a team is applying Team Sync, they have the potential to create a sum greater than their individual efforts. A *five*-capacity team member is no longer limited to his or her Personal Capacity or personal knowledge. The knowledge that is available to the *ten* is now fully available to the *five,* and the knowledge available to the *five* is fully available to the *ten*!

When Team Sync is applied over a long enough period of time, we begin to see the real benefits! No longer is a person limited by their own Personal Capacity. They now have available to them the skill, the wisdom, and the competence of the rest of the team, producing the potential for an increased Personal Capacity! Notice the increased capacity of several members of our team.

$$5 \times 5 \times 10 \times 5 \times 5 = 6{,}250$$
$$7 \times 5 \times 10 \times 6 \times 5 = 10{,}500$$

This increased capacity was partially the result of personal development by each individual team member, but Team Sync played a vital role as well. Team Sync created a place where thoughts, concepts, insights, and strategies could be shared and investigated in a safe environment. Environments where creativity is celebrated! In such environments, everyone has the potential and freedom to add their personal contribution towards achieving the team's overall objectives. A place where individuals are lifted, not put down.

19

LIFE LESSONS

Life Lessons that increase your Personal Capacity

Many people have asked me the secrets of my success. Really, it's hard to put your finger on any one thing that creates success. But if I had to pick one area, I would say it was the life application lessons I learned from my father. My father helped me see and understand the Kingdom of God. Here are a couple of examples.

(1) The blessing or the curse that you decide

Over and over again my father would say, "Son, a person cannot touch a man or woman of God with the words of their mouth and not have it affect them every time." You will be affected either in a positive way or a negative way, but know this—the words of your mouth will have an effect. He would say, "Son, many people think that God turns a deaf ear as they tear down His ministers." Sadly, they are mistaken. They will be affected every time! People think that they are getting away with something, but they are forfeiting the full blessing of God in their lives. *We only see what is; God knows what could have been!*

You cannot touch a man or woman of God with the words of your mouth in a negative way and not have it affect you every time.

My father told me this hundreds of times in my life. People ask me how I ended up working with hundreds of pastors around the world. Why do hundreds of pastors trust me with their intimate thoughts and details of their lives and ministries? The truth is that my mom and dad modeled such a love, honor, and respect for the pastor's ministry office. I guess it shouldn't be such a surprise that I have dedicated my life to the building up and support of pastors. If you think about it, far too many people talk freely about what they like and don't like about their pastor and their church. Often their children or others are listening. Those seeds will grow up and produce a harvest. When those negative seeds produce their fruit in your children's lives, you blame the devil but God's looking at you!

LIFE LESSON

(2) Faithfulness alone is highly overrated

For the past five years, Tammy and I have traveled around the world helping churches. Many pastors have given us the nickname "The Problem Solvers for Pastors." We seem to have the ability to help churches through tough challenges. Often these challenges are due to faithful people. Many pastors are bitten by faithful people.

The truth is that faithfulness alone is highly overrated. You might be the most faithful usher in the church. For twenty years, you worked faithfully in every service. There is a plaque on the church wall as a tribute to your faithfulness. But that does not make you loyal. You could be faithful to show up for every service for twenty years but steal one hundred dollars out of the offering before it is counted!

Most people do not understand that faithfulness is all about *action*, but loyalty is a condition and *position of the heart!*

If a man comes home every night after work and does not kick the dog, he is considered faithful. However, if he has fantasies about being physically intimate with other women, he may be faithful, but he is not loyal. He has faithful actions but not a loyal heart. A faithful man with a disloyal heart catches many women totally off their guard.

Personally, I love dogs. I guess you could call me a dog lover. When I was growing up, I had a collie named Stormy. He was the best dog a boy could have. The two of us went on many wonderful adventures together. The old saying, "A dog is man's best friend," was true in this case.

One morning when I was very young, Stormy and I were bringing in the herd of milk cows from the back forty. Then from out of nowhere came a pack of wild dogs. When I first noticed the dogs coming in our direction, I didn't feel like I was in danger. But Stormy thought otherwise. He began to bark and growl. He started to push on my legs, as if to say, "Run!" And that is exactly what I did. Our back forty was over one mile from our home. I think I ran a four-minute mile that day. I remember looking back over my shoulder, seeing Stormy in a fight with six or eight wild dogs.

When I got to the barn, I told my father what had happened. Immediately, my father grabbed our model 94 Winchester rifle, and we climbed into our old green farm truck and started for the back forty. When we arrived, there was no sign of Stormy or the wild dogs. But there was blood everywhere. Then out of the corner of my eye I saw something — it was Stormy. He was a real mess! He was covered in blood, with deep gashes all over his body. There was no doubt in this boy's mind that Stormy had saved my life. Stormy lived for at least ten more years. But from that day forward, he limped everywhere he went. Stormy was a loyal and faithful friend.

After Stormy died, I purchased a new dog. He seemed like a great dog. He acted just like Stormy. He was a faithful friend. But one day when I was feeding him, he moved his dinner dish into the middle of the doorway. So I reached down to move the dish out of the doorway. I could not believe what happened next. That dog bit me on the hand. I could not believe what was happening. Somehow that dog thought I wanted his dog chow. That dog turned out to be very faithful when it came to guarding the house and being there for every meal. But he turned out to not be very loyal.

Faithfulness does not produce loyalty! However, loyalty will normally produce faithfulness!

Many pastors and leaders are bitten by faithful people when they mistake faithfulness for loyalty. They do not understand that faithfulness does not produce loyalty. But loyalty will most always produce a level of faithfulness. I have been praying the same prayer for the past twenty-two years, "Lord help me to be a loyal husband, help me be a loyal father, help me be loyal to my pastor and my church, and help me to be loyal to Your Kingdom." I believe my loyalty has produced a faithfulness that has resulted in an Increased Capacity in my life!

CHAPTER
20

PERSONAL CAPACITY:
THE JOURNEY OF A LIFETIME

I remember so clearly the day I became aware of my need to increase my Personal Capacity. Somehow, life had placed me in a do-or-die situation. I had been promoted repeatedly until one day I was clearly incompetent. I remember how excited my family and friends were as we celebrated each new promotion. I received more money, more influence, better hours, the best office, and a private car space. But little did we know that each new promotion drove me closer to my Failing Point.

The problem was the combination of a growing organization and regular promotions based on faithfulness, not skill and competence. At times, the pressure was almost more than I could bear. I knew that if I didn't do something quickly, my financial future was on the line. The thought of telling my wife and children that we may be forced to move from our home for financial reasons caused me to plan my escape. But thank God I didn't run. I got serious about increasing my capacity.

I want to give you a few final thoughts as you chart your course for a greater capacity.

(1) Increasing your Personal Capacity is not a destination; it is a journey.

I guess if I had to tell you the most important key I have learned, it would be that increasing your Personal Capacity is not a destination; it is a journey. The year I set out to increase my capacity changed my life. Within one year, I was not only competent in my position but Next-Level competent. That year, I increased my financial compensation over 300 percent. What a great feeling it was to move from a place of incompetence to a place of competence. However, I quickly learned that increasing my capacity was not an event but a lifelong journey.

The quality of your life is being determined by your Personal Capacity, and your Personal Capacity will determine your destiny.

(2) No one thing will bring success. You must engage "Life Sync."

It did not take long for me to realize that no one thing would give me the results I desired. I remember the frustration I felt when I realized that I had increased my capacity to the next level, but my habits were still on the previous level. My old habits were like a gravitational pull towards my previous level. Day after day, it was a showdown between my habits and me. And honestly, I continued losing the war on my habits until I developed the process of Next-Level Habits. If you're going to navigate successfully the Personal Capacity Journey, then you must simultaneously integrate multiple areas of personal growth. I call this process Life Sync.

(3) There are actions you could take, but first, you must make a decision.

Increasing your Personal Capacity starts with a decision followed by corresponding actions. You must make the decision to stop blaming the quality of your life on your gender, your skin color, your ethnic origin, your financial status, or even your geographic location. You must take responsibility for the fact that the quality of your life is a direct result of your Personal Capacity. Next, you must take action steps towards increasing your capacity.

(4) Do not be ashamed of the FAITH in your heart.

I have discovered that many people live out their lives far below their Personal Capacity because of a fear of what others will think or say. When you accept or receive negative statements from people, you empower those words. We all know what it feels like to have someone laugh at our plans and/or our desires. Statements like, "You cannot be serious. You think you could ever do that!" Teenagers are often told, "You'll never amount to anything with your attitude." After a person is laughed at a few times, they begin to hide the desires of their heart. But I cannot encourage you enough to not be ashamed of the faith in your heart. Pick out your destination, chart your course, develop your action steps, and set sail for a greater capacity.

(5) Quit calling your fear "common sense."

Learn how to recognize intimidation in your life and deny its control. We all hear the voice of intimidation, but we must not give in to it. Here is a question you must answer, "What are the voices of intimidation that I need to resist or silence?" These voices of intimidation are hindering you from increasing your capacity. Remember, never act under the influence of intimidation. More importantly, never allow intimidation to stop you from moving forward. We all have the opportunity to speak from our fear or our intimidation, but you need to choose to speak from the faith in your heart.

I love the story of Gideon. When God said to him, "You mighty man of valor," Gideon found the words of God hard to believe. It was clear that God looked at him in a greater capacity than Gideon looked at himself. God boldly declared, "This is what I want to do in your life." The problem was not how God viewed Gideon, but how Gideon viewed himself. Truthfully, many of us are just like Gideon; we continually point towards what we view as our lack of Personal Capacity but God continually points towards what He knows as our potential capacity.

The problem is not how God views you but how you view yourself.

At first, Gideon found it hard to believe in himself because of his mind-set. A mind-set is simply a preconditioned way of thinking. A person's mind-set or preconditioned thinking will cause them not to think a new thought that will create a better future. Gideon overcame his insecurities and accomplished significant things after he changed his thinking.

I have one final question for you. How are all men equal? They all have the same amount of time. So what makes the difference? It's not just putting in time; it's what you put into the time that makes the difference. Don't wait another day to begin increasing your Personal Capacity. Assume full responsibility for your personal

> It's not just putting in time; it's what you put into the time that makes the difference.

development. The reward is the fulfillment of the dream deep in your heart. Increasing your Personal Capacity is the journey of a lifetime.

About the Author

Eddie and his wife, Tammy, are two of the most unique leaders in the Kingdom today. Together they empower leaders and pastors around the world. In 1997, after seventeen years of full-time ministry the Windsor family moved to England and began working with pastors and speaking life into the churches. The churches are hungry and are rising up to the challenge of building a relevant, healthy and significant house of worship.

Eddie has founded the Media Broadcasting Group, The Media Outreach Network, and has grown his mentor and modeling group, The Leadership Viewpoint, to over three hundred pastors across England. He also hosts conferences that coach, inspire and build pastors and leaders to reach their full potential.

The Windsors also travel worldwide speaking, teaching and training leaders in all positions of leadership whether in ministry or business. Eddie is a real, bottom-line, practical teacher and his teaching style will increase the capacity of anyone aspiring to go to the next level. He is passionate about seeing pastors discover and fulfill their vision and destiny in strength and confidence. Eddie was raised in a home where respect and honor for the house of God and the man of God, was strongly taught. His greatest strength has become teaching that principle. Pastors have begun to nickname Eddie, a pastor to pastors.

Eddie, Tammy and their two children, Daniel and Bethany, lived in England for over four years. Daniel and Bethany are now high school graduates living in Tacoma, Washington. Daniel is headed off to college for a career in

Media, while Bethany is also completing her first year of Wisdom for Life Leadership School and will finish her second year in 2004. Eddie and Tammy continue to minister in England over six months of the year.

Eddie speaks at churches, conferences, business and executive meetings, and is an excellent staff strategist and trainer.

CONTACT AND RESOURCE INFORMATION:

Eddie and Tammy Windsor
1819 E. 72nd St.
Tacoma, WA 98404

Phone: 253.475.6454 Ext: 214

Email: EDDIE@EDDIEWINDSOR.ORG

Web site: WWW.EDDIEWINDSOR.ORG